The Earth at Our Doorstep

The Earth at Our Doorstep

Contemporary Writers Celebrate the Landscapes of Home

Edited by Annie Stine

SIERRA CLUB BOOKS *San Francisco*

The Sierra Club, founded in 1892 by John Muir, has devoted itself to the study and protection of the earth's scenic and ecological resources—mountains, wetlands, woodlands, wild shores and rivers, deserts and plains. The publishing program of the Sierra Club offers books to the public as a nonprofit educational service in the hope that they may enlarge the public's understanding of the Club's basic concerns. The point of view expressed in each book, however, does not necessarily represent that of the Club. The Sierra Club has some sixty chapters coast to coast, in Canada, Hawaii, and Alaska. For information about how you may participate in its programs to preserve wilderness and the quality of life, please address inquiries to Sierra Club, 730 Polk Street, San Francisco, CA 94109.

Library of Congress Cataloging-in-Publication Data
The earth at our doorstep : contemporary writers celebrate the landscapes of
    home / edited by Annie Stine.
        p.   cm.
    ISBN 0-87156-381-9 (pbk. : alk. paper)
    1. Landscape—United States.   2. Home—United States.
    3. Human ecology—United States.   I. Stine, Annie.
    GF503.E37   1996
    304.2'3—dc20   95-39902
                                                                        CIP

Production by Robin Rockey
Cover design by David Bullen Design
Book design by David Bullen Design
Composition by Wilsted & Taylor
Printed in the United States of America on acid-free paper containing a minimum of 50% recovered waste paper, of which at least 10% of the fiber content is post-consumer waste

10   9   8   7   6   5   4   3   2   1

For my parents, Betty and Harold Stine,
who kept the light on;
and for Phil, my partner on this delicate arch

Contents

ix   *Contents*

Acknowledgments

Many people have come to my aid and comfort during the years of this book's evolution, people open of heart and keen of ear. Special thanks to my soulmates Sally Benjamin and Ronnie Jacobs, who gave me a home when I first landed on this unfamiliar coast; to my colleagues at *Sierra* magazine: Jonathan King, Joan Hamilton, Paul Rauber, Reed McManus, Marc Mardon, Marc Lecard, and Bob Schildgen, the finest of editors with whom I shared the finest days; to my slickrock pal Catherine Fox, who witnessed the big change; to Elizabeth Wray and Wendy Lichtman for their love, humor, and graceful manipulation of the first person singular; to Kathy Evers for her prayers and rescues; to my brother Peter, who always believed; and to Sierra Club Books editors Barbara Ras and Jim Cohee, whose faith and encouragement helped me get to the right place at the right time. Finally, love and gratitude to Colin Kelly and Phil Greenberg, with whom I am safely home, no matter where we are.

Introduction

This is a collection of love stories. They are accounts of arrival and departure, of expectation and acceptance, of mutual dependence and transformation. There is great tenderness here, and generosity. And true to all love stories, there is the shadow of potential loss.

I did not think of these essays this way when I began soliciting them for *Sierra* magazine six years ago. My fellow editors and I wanted to explore the environmental implications of how people live, motivated in part by the desire to inspire rather than depress our readers, and in part by the belief that the choices we make about food and shelter, play and work, ultimately have as profound an effect on our futures as do the whims of faraway bureaucrats. I proposed a column called

"Whereabouts," for which I would ask writers to reflect on where they lived and why they lived there. After a few years I realized that in addition to containing dozens of pieces that stood wonderfully on their own, my "Whereabouts" file drawer held a unique rendering of the American landscape, a loving narrative of the intricate relationships we build with the places we make our homes.

The story begins with how we came to live where we do. Sometimes it was an event beyond our control and only temporarily memorable: the money ran out, the partner ran off. Sometimes the reason was utilitarian: a job, a school. Sometimes it was an inner, less communicable need: we felt pulled to the shadows—or the light—of the country, or to the light—or the shadows—of the city. Maybe it had something to do with the way the moon lifted itself so calmly over the hill, making us want to stay to see it one more time, and then another. Or perhaps after many years of speaking an unfamiliar language we woke up one day really wanting to go to a tag sale, not a garage sale, to eat a submarine, not a hoagie, and so we packed up and headed back to where we were born and raised. Or maybe, although less often in these restless times of boundless mobility, we never left at all.

The contributors to this book followed these various paths leading home. The poet Donald Hall tells of how, after years of living in the "relentless thin suburban present, disconnected from the past, looking toward an illusory compensatory future," he returned to rural New Hampshire, the land of his grandparents and his great-grandparents, to help preserve in words the stories of his cousins and neighbors. When he was an adolescent living in Washington, D.C., John Daniel decided that Oregon must be the wildest place on Earth; he headed there at eighteen and has not strayed far for almost thirty years. All it took was a cloud to drop from a mountain to convince Lynne Bama to change her life and move to Wyoming.

We do not always make our homes in the lands of our younger dreams. We settle; as we come to rest, we also compromise. We might have pictured ourselves standing at the edge of the wild gray Pacific, but now we sit on the bank of a still brown pond in the middle of the continent. Although we may have wanted to whisper on a porch swing in our sleeveless blouses on August nights, instead we watch the freezing summer fog erase the city block by block. But with this settling begins the richer part of the story. It is with the unfolding of months and years, when we become a regular at the neighborhood creek or coffee shop, that we surprise ourselves by becoming who we never thought we'd be, or who we always knew we were.

So it was for many of the writers here, who often landed in a setting quite different from what they had once imagined for themselves. Sue Halpern, who had always thought she would end up in a house on stilts above a rocky sea, moved inland for love and made a home among the bears and lakes of the Adirondacks. Steeped in the traditions of the Northeast and Europe, W. S. Merwin never thought he would live in the tropics, or tend to the gardens and the rains, the politics and the cultures of the Pacific. Both bear witness to the fact that a landscape changes not only how we see and what we need, but who we are.

The writers in this collection also give testimony to another truth: to sustain a landscape requires constant care, for the developers are never far from our homes. In his account of how a committed inhabitant of the Sierra Nevada foothills must perpetually navigate among those who would survey and log and build, Gary Snyder notes that "there is no place, no matter how remote, where the dialectic of exploitation and conservation is not at play."

In the years I spent editing "Whereabouts" for *Sierra,* I always had the hope (a helpful one for an editor) that for the writers the assignment was more of a reprieve than a task, a chance for them to sit in the kitchen with memories and motives and chat for a while. If that was in fact the case—and many contributors told me it was—then we as readers can consider ourselves graciously invited to join the conversation.

For many of the writers here, home is as rich with people as it is with mountains, trees, or sky. Soon others drift over to our table. Through Brenda Peterson we meet the wrinkled old woman who feeds the gulls and the faithful taxi driver who obligingly tears the bread. On a different coast, Garrett Bauman wanders in from the midnight snow and introduces us to the blind woman who taught him how to recognize an oriole.

As Pam Houston searches for her own home, she contemplates the homeless and those awkward, aching encounters that are part of every urban dweller's daily life.

It is intimacy, the feeling of warmth as we clasp our cups of tea, that give these essays their felicity and power. The writers are not expounding on abstract theories of home or place; rather they are offering the sights that welcome them each morning, the sounds that accompany their daily work, the smells that rise from the earth at the doorstep, the folks who give comfort along the way.

Like the best of love stories, these essays are quietly instructive. As geographies they give us another way of thinking about islands, ridgetops, and valleys. They help us watch the slow things, to celebrate the perennials that return and to mourn the migrating birds that do not. They remind us of what fragile and enduring gifts we have been given, and how temporary is our sojourn among them. And finally, they move us to consider and tend to our own homes—to the land they rest on, and to the selves that reside in their many rooms.

Annie Stine

The Earth at Our Doorstep

W. S. Merwin

Living on an Island

BY NOW THERE are three pieces of ordinary personal information, plain details of the sort that one is asked daily to supply on questionnaires, toward which I continue to feel a certain wariness. This is so even though I consider all of these facts to be manifestations of good fortune and certainly I would not change any of them.

Occupation. If you have grown up in this language and society you do not simply say, with no sense of the possible consequences, that you are a poet. But the public and private reverberations of that one are existential and this is not the occasion to consider them. The other two are geographical, whatever that means.

Address. I have lived now for a quarter of my life in Hawaii, on what has been called for well over a hundred years one of the outer islands. I live in the country, on the windward, rainy side of Maui, at some distance from a dirt road that leads to the edge of a sea cliff. There is no other roof in sight, only a deep valley full of tall trees, and beyond them an open promontory above the Pacific, in which there is no other land between here and Alaska.

The post office six miles away, with its single star route which a few years ago was said to be the longest in the country, serves the scattered district of Haiku. These days the name is generally written the way I have just written it, and most people pronounce it "highcoo." If they are doing the asking, and are of a friendly and literary turn, they are apt to assume that the name refers to the seventeen-syllable Japanese verse form, and they may suggest that there must be some connection between having such an occupation and living in a place with such a name.

But in fact the name Haiku is not Japanese at all, and though its origin is unknown, there is no doubt that it is really two Hawaiian words: *ha'i* (with a glottal stop between the vowels), which in English means "break," and *ku,* "erect, straight up." Mary Kawena Pukui in her *Place Names of Hawaii* says the name Ha'i ku translates as "speak abruptly" or "sharp break." Here it may refer to the steep-sided ravines that wind down the skirts of the mountain to the cliffs. They are watercourses that are almost impassable: tumbled, rocky, green, shadowy, ferny, and secret. The enterprising Caucasians of the nineteenth century christened them gulches and considered them unprofitable nuisances. Developers and roadbuilders regard them as obstacles. They cradle—they are—the least touched, least exploited presences in the region. These ravines are a direct link with the island's past (every watercourse on the coast has not only its Hawaiian name but its own legends), with its botanical and geological origins, its native self. What has happened to the name *Ha'i ku* is consistent with the recent history of this *hamakua loa,* this "long corner" of the coast.

Then there are the questions that come to hover around the statement that I live in Hawaii at all, if the information is given to someone who lives somewhere else. Often there is a certain startled incredulity. Do you *really* live there? Do you really *live* there? (It may be partly just that it is becoming rare to live anywhere, as localities become prefabricated and generic, and people feel that they live less in places than in situations.) And then questions testing the credibility of such a statement, often beginning with "How long have you lived there?" Assuming—quite rightly in my case—that I was not born here, that I must not have been born here, that I must have come here from the world, and that my being here is a matter of choice. Then, in one form or another: Why? Questions revealing, along with helpless disbelief, shades of envy and at times some form or another of resentment. Naive or sophisticated, most of the questions disclose an underlying conviction that the Hawaiian Islands are in some way unreal.

Part of this can be ascribed to the image broadcast with increasing effect in the course of this century by the tourist business: the cliche, the poster world of beaches, sunsets, brownskinned beauties wearing flowers (non-Hawaiian flowers), and so on. It certainly would be surprising to be told that someone from the real world of air-conditioning, commuting, pollution, debts, and the rest of the news, had gone to *live* there. But long before that counterfeit image became current, a particularly European and American view of things set civilization, science, industry, cities, virtue, God, cleanliness, and reality on one side, and primitivism, idleness, heathenism, ignorance, sensuality, iniquity, error, and unreality on the other. The belief system that encouraged such a division was a self-serving, deadly credo, and it has not gone away or grown less toxic.

I had run across this credo through years of pulling back and forth between the city and what we still call the country. Much of the world I had grown up in insisted that the country, whatever the word referred to, was essentially less real than the city, and when I returned from it, sooner or later someone was sure to welcome me back to the real world. I had worked that one out for myself, more or less, by the time I came to Hawaii, but it never occurred to me that I would live in the tropics, and even after I was here it seemed unlikely at first that I would stay.

Lawrence Durrell begins one of his books about the Mediterranean with a passage about *islomania,* the addiction to islands, and the addict who at last finds his island. Afterward, everything is bound to follow from that, and the attachment to a place and a set of geographical circumstances is really no more rational or available to analysis than any other attraction or affection or recognition. But one can point to how such things seem to have started, what appears to have set them off and seems to nourish them, noticing as one does so how partial, in every sense, such indications are.

A love of the tropics is bound to be physical, influenced by an unfathomable response to the flood of sunlight, the massive rains, the air itself. For me the attraction was part of a continuing gravitation toward the neighborhood of trees and mountains, rainforests, dry forests, mountain ridges, and sea cliffs. I am aware of how little I can say about them and the predilection for them, and often I would rather say nothing at all.

Gardening is another kind of relation with living things, and one that I have missed whenever I have not had it. Here I can garden all year round, and grow, among other things, plants native to the place; and there are good reasons, apart from the pleasure of it, for doing so. In gardening, as my wife and I go about it here, what are called concerns—for ecology and the environment, for example—merge inevitably with work done every day, within sight of the house, with our own hands, and the concerns remain intimate and familiar rather than abstract and far away. They do not have to be thought about, they are at home in the mind. I have never lived anywhere where that was more true.

As for history, and the sense of human venture and time, I

grew up with the assumption that the center of it was the American Northeast and its European motherland. But it is the civilizations circling the Pacific, as well as Latin America, that I turn to increasingly. Living in Hawaii has helped effect that turn of attention.

In my case it has also been the working out of an affinity. From childhood on I have been drawn to people of other racial backgrounds, to indigenous and oral cultures. The presence of a Hawaiian tradition, however depleted and damaged, and the discovery of the cultures of the Pacific, are inseparable from my deepening feelings for the islands themselves. Before I had been here very long Hawaii felt to me like a center of such things, which in turn seemed to be directly related to local issues. Development, for instance, was usually by one set of people at the expense of another and of the natural world, which again and again was a victim of the same motives that were destroying it everywhere. The defense of it locally was clearly inseparable from a fidelity to it as a whole.

Things here are on a scale that seems human. And living on an island, in the country, in our time, is a constant reminder of the finite condition of the natural world, and of what, from a narrow point of view, are commonly referred to as "resources." There is only so much coast, so much of anything. It is easy to be aware that everyone is living on an island.

Then there are those who ask what relation there is between living in a place such as this and what I manage to write. But for that one, I'm still trying to find the answer myself.

Pam Houston

A Word in Someone Else's Mouth

I LOOK OUT MY window this morning and see that my backyard is, against all probability, Oakland, California. I've been in Oakland exactly a year now, a long time for a country girl living in the city for the very first time. I came here for a love that went almost immediately sour, then surprised myself by staying, something goatish in me unwilling to leave this landscape until I find out what there is here I might learn to call home.

It's a common problem for me, confusing man with land, romance with landscape, cowboys with the canyons and mesas on which they ride. In the end it boils down to a simple figure-ground relationship. Once the man steps out of the photo the scenery moves forward and becomes what there is left to love. Or perhaps it is my loving the backdrop that allows the man to step into the photo in the first place, trouble coming only when I realize he's blocked my view.

What I know for sure is that my first true love was the land I saw around me: light snow falling on the stubbled remains of a Pennsylvania cornfield, the fiery light of a late afternoon in September across the fragile dune and grassland of the Jersey Shore. As I got older it seemed that each time life taught me something about love it gave me an even more dramatic landscape on which to try it out: the perfect turquoise translucence of the water over the Bahama Banks, the deep banded labyrinths of Utah's endlessly repeating canyon country, a winter helicopter tour over Alaska's St. Elias Glacier, that forever country of granite, sky, and ice.

When I turned twenty-one I got on my bicycle one day in New Jersey and didn't get off until Grand Lake, Colorado, and it was then I fell in love with the Rocky Mountains once and forever. Last year I consummated that love by buying a little ranch just the other side of the Continental Divide at nine thousand feet in a town I so far won't mention the name of in public. The ranch has elk in the backyard in the winter and blue columbine growing wild on the hillsides in summer, no light pollution for miles in all directions, and the best view of the Milky Way in the lower forty-eight, the air so high and thin and guarded as it is by the Great Divide. There's not a traffic light in the entire county; sometimes several days go by without a car driving down my road.

I bought the ranch right about the same time I moved to Oakland, and though I know it makes lousy sense financially, I was following a different line of reason. It was knowing that ranch was there waiting for me that allowed me to give the city a try, to live for the first time ever in a place where I own a key to my house, a place where I have to lock my doors, a place so unnatural the only real threat comes from members of my own species, a place where I have had to learn to pay attention in an entirely different way.

As a writer it is my job to become an instant expert on a series of momentary backyards, to be able to look out the window at Puerto López, Ecuador, or Hay-on-Wye, Wales, or Bettles, Alaska, or Georgetown, Great Exuma, or Val-Les-Bains, France, and to take them in, to imagine a life in them, to memorize and appropriate them, to make them mine. What I trade for this pleasure is the concept of "home," a word in someone else's mouth, remote to me and foreign as the moon, a word whose very presence on the page sets me trembling with longing.

It hasn't therefore come as any surprise to me that I have fallen a little in love with my new home in California, with its gentle madrone and eucalyptus hills, with the white city across the bay that sparkles brighter even than the sparkling water, with the elegant fingers of the Golden Gate, and the wild wide ocean that lies beyond.

Even Oakland has caught me with her particular beauty, the yellow lights that twinkle and bob around the shore of Lake Merritt, the hydraulic lifts that stand over the industrial harbor like giant Doberman pinschers guarding the freighters, my little house nestled high in the oak trees with an almost-view of the bay.

More than the sights, it's the smells and the sounds and the energy of this place that have hooked me: fresh blueberry muffins at the Oakland Grill down on Fourth Street, the train whistle sounding right out the front door, and tattooed men of all colors unloading crates of cauliflower, broccoli, and peas. Or the particular buzz of the Housewife's Market on Ninth and Clay: the hanging pig quarters at Allan's Ham and Bacon; the African and Cajun spice store; Maura's fresh fish market; and the girl in the center of it all who makes fresh banana milkshakes and tells everyone for free how happy they ought to be to be alive.

There's Quinn's down on Embarcadero, where, if you make it through the neighborhoods you have to drive through to get there, you are rewarded with the good company of drunken sailors, a floor inches deep in peanut shells, and on Thursday nights sea chanteys performed live and well into the drunken wee hours. And my favorite, the Alley Bar on Grand Avenue, where Rod Dibble has sat at the piano for thirty-nine years and where on any given evening almost every type of person you can imagine comes through the door, sits at the piano bar, and eventually bursts into song. From the ex–Oakland Raider who renders "Black Magic" without ever once opening his eyes, to the computer salesman who'll bring you to tears with his "Old Man River," to a rousing rendition of "42nd Street," for which the rhythm section consists of everyone in the place tap dancing their quarters across the bar. The Alley is the best night out in Oakland, maybe in America, maybe in the world.

Oakland is a place alive with stories, with the constant clash and intersection of so many disparate lives, tragic and joyful, empty and brimming, all in such unnatural and dangerous proximity. I would be a fool to leave before my time.

I was eating in a fancy French restaurant not long ago with two friends—it was a night full of laughter and ideas and we lingered over our last glass of wine so long that the maitre'd finally asked us to leave. As we walked down the front steps into the street a homeless man approached us. He had deep black skin, an old down jacket, and a knitted Raiders' cap pulled tightly over his ears.

"I've been watching you through the window," he said. "I've been waiting. Could any of you spare a dime?"

We dug through our pockets and came up with two dollars and change.

"That's wonderful. Thank you, God bless you," he said. "Now, would you like to hear me recite Robert Frost's 'Stopping by Woods on a Snowy Evening'?"

And then he recited it, and rather well.

"Now," he said, "could I try out a little of my improvisational poetry on you?"

I suppose you could argue that everyone, everywhere, has a story. What's different in Oakland is that everybody's willing to *share*.

And you've got to love a city that won't give you the easy break. Like the morning just after I'd arrived last year when I found myself at the Peet's Coffee on Lake Shore Drive.

It was a Sunday in mid-January, rainy, dank, and cold, the kind of day when you understand exactly how a city of more than a million people can be the loneliest place on earth. I got out of the house to keep from drowning in my own isolation, popped the Counting Crows in the tape deck, and went to see the skinny guy with the dreadlocks who I believe makes the best latte this side of Seattle. I told him as much and made him smile, no small feat in that kind of weather.

As I was leaving the shop a little girl approached me, all dimples and pleats and braids.

"Excuse me, ma'am," she said. "Would you like to buy some Girl Scout cookies?"

Redemption, I thought. Perhaps Oakland is not another planet after all.

"I'd love to," I said, "but I really don't eat cookies. Thank you so much for asking, though."

The little girl turned on her heel, moved toward her mother, and said, "Well in that case you can go to hell."

Two more homeless stories:

I was having yet another bad day, love-wise, but I had front-row seats to Van Morrison that night. I got all dressed up in a sheer, ivory-colored skirt and a long sweater, navy pumps, and for me, big hair.

I was walking to the bar where I would meet my friends before the show, more like stalking really, head down, engaged in a little self-talk.

"Get over it," I was saying. "He's old and balding and he has bad shoes and you better damn well have fun tonight despite him." I was so preoccupied I hardly noticed the young man on crutches I stepped over, the unshaven but pleasant face, the rusted coffee can beside him.

"I don't even want any money from you," he said. "I'd just like you to smile."

I stopped in my tracks and grinned down at him.

"See," he said, "it's easy when you stop trying so hard."

I giggled all the way to the end of the block, where I turned around, walked back to him, and gave him all the money in my wallet, about eighteen bucks.

"Use that line again," I said. "It's a killer."

I took my place in the front row at Van Morrison and danced my heart out all night long.

And the last:

I was at the late show at the Grand Lake Theater one Tuesday night. It's one of those magnificent old movie houses with a huge marquee that lights up the sky like a carnival, a ceiling that looks like it belongs in a Spanish cathedral, heavy red velvet curtains laced with threads that sparkle gold, and a real live piano player who disappears into the floor when the previews begin. I like to linger there when the movie's over, watch the credits and the artificial stars sparkling in the ceiling. That evening I was the last person to step out of the theater into a chilly and deserted night.

I had one foot off the curb when the man first approached me, a little too close for comfort even then.

"Do you have any change you could spare?" he said.

The truth was I didn't. I had scraped the bottom of my purse to put together enough quarters, nickels, and dimes to get into the movie, and the guy behind the glass had let me in thirty-three cents short.

I said I was sorry and headed for the parking lot. I knew he was behind me, but I didn't turn around. I should have gotten my keys out before I left the theater, I thought. Shouldn't have stayed to see every credit roll.

About ten steps from my car I felt a firm jab in the middle of my rib cage.

"I bet you'd feel differently," the man said, "if I had a gun in my hand."

I was having—big surprise—another bad day, and I was in just enough of a mood to turn on him.

"I might feel differently," I said, "but I still wouldn't have any money."

He flinched almost imperceptibly, changed the angle of his body, just slightly back and away, and in that change I saw the bigger change, from aggression to defense. Oakland was not unlike the Rocky Mountains in that moment, the man not unlike the bears I'd run into there.

And when he moved his body, when his eyes dropped from mine to his hand holding whatever it was in his jacket pocket, I was reminded of a time I almost walked into a female grizz with a nearly grown cub. How we had stood there posturing a moment, how she had glanced down at her cub just that way, given me the opportunity to let her know she didn't need to kill me, that we could both just go on our way.

"Look," I said. "I've had a really emotional day, okay?" As I talked I dug into my purse and grabbed my set of keys, which with the ranch and my house and the three cars I have the use of, five different jobs, and storage units all over America, is a kind of a weapon in its own right. "And I really think you ought to just let me get in my car and go home."

While he considered this I took the last steps to my car and got in. I didn't look in the rearview mirror until I was on the freeway.

I was flying the puddle jumper from Portland, Oregon, home to Oakland last week when our California-based pilot came over the loud speaker just as we reached 39,000 feet.

"Good morning, folks," he said. "Our flight today is going to take us over Grants Pass and the Kalmiopsis Wilderness, slightly to the west of Mount Shasta, through the Trinity Alps, then over the Coast Range to Point Reyes, the Golden Gate Bridge, and the Oakland Airport."

He paused before continuing.

"Unfortunately, our cloud layer is going to preclude your seeing any of that, so you are just going to have to sit back, close your eyes, and visualize those beautiful landmarks in your mind."

A little alternative therapy with our coffee and muffin, free of charge, California style, I thought. But I did what he said. I visualized those places, and others, the dark streets and the mean streets and the street where I got hustled by a little girl, a ratty bear in one hand, a dripping ice cream in the other. She dropped the bear long enough to put her hand out to me and when I asked how much she needed, she just said, "How much you got?"

And I thought about the intersection of our two lives in that moment, how I felt homeless by virtue of having too many choices, how she must have felt having too few. And I knew why I would always give her whatever money I had on me, and knew also why it would never be enough. And I wanted a home right then more than ever, stuck in the embarrassment and shame of privilege, and I vowed to make myself a home somehow, if only because I *could*.

I don't get out to my ranch as often as I would like to. The closest airport is a four-hour drive in good weather, it's another day bringing the house to life, and the longer I stay in

Oakland, the quicker my schedule seems to fill up. For now I just sit and listen to the helicopters overhead each night and know that somewhere along the Continental Divide is a place where there is utter silence. I sit in the twenty-four-hour traffic snarl where the interstates meet and know that all day in Colorado no one has driven down my road. And I know just as well the fickle nature of my longing. If I were in Colorado I'd sit in the middle of all that rock and ponderosa splendor and yearn for bookstores and lattes, for sushi and the sea.

I'll get this thing called "home" right one day, love too, I hope, a landscape where I can stand in the photo next to a man, the scenery behind us, both of us clear-eyed and looking out. For now those pages of my life wait unoccupied, rooms in a log-hewn ranch house, while I spin around and around the globe, collecting landscapes, attaching names and faces, places I've been for a moment or several—Oakland—long enough at least to hear the strange and hungry cadence of a streetwise Robert Frost and the unexpected comfort of a song from the Alley Bar.

Sue Halpern

A Mind of Winter

A FEW WEEKS into autumn and it is snowing in the
Adirondacks, bowing the hardwoods and fleecing
the tamaracks, which lately have turned to yellow.
No one who lives in these mountains would call this weather
unseasonable: every landscape has its season, when the angle
of light, the folds of the earth, the particular array of colors
seem to bless and complete it, and here that season is winter,
whenever it arrives. In winter the Adirondacks secede without
declaration, remove themselves from civilization as if their entire 6 million acres were on retreat. The acoustics become
rounder, the forests open up. There are two dominant colors,
white and green, and no apparent need for any other.

Had I first seen these mountains in May or September, it is

possible I would think that the damp new leaves of spring or the spectacle of fall best displayed their contours. But I first saw them in November, when the trees were stripped to the bark and the frozen ground seemed to call for snow as if it were a vocation. And then it did snow, and the world grew still and settled into its skin. "One must have a mind of winter / To regard the frost and the boughs / Of the pine trees crusted with snow / . . . and not to think / Of any misery in the sound of the wind . . . ," Wallace Stevens writes. And so it is with me.

I did not mean to move to the mountains to make a home and a life. My husband brought me here, only he wasn't my husband then, the house we stayed in wasn't yet our house, and I had no idea that it ever would be. On the map the place we were going that weekend was called Adirondack Park. At the time, I was living in New York City, and as I understood it, Central Park was a park, because as much as you might want to, you couldn't live there. But here I was, five hours north of Manhattan, in a wilderness as untamed and vast and separate as any imaginable, shared by bears and coyotes and eagles and herons and people alike. What was unimaginable was becoming one of those people.

"It's so far," my friends who lived in places like Boston and New York would say of the Adirondacks, and for a while I knew exactly what they were talking about—the 250 miles between. But after a time I began to understand that the true measure of distance is not feet or miles, but proximity to the things you value or need. The night sky, say. Or a field of Indian paintbrush. Or a house in the lee of a mountain. By then I had been living in that house a year or two.

In a way, it is the presence of people, as much as that of peregrine falcons or certain rare varieties of arctic moss, or the Adirondacks' sheer size, that makes this place unique. Adirondack Park is an experiment in cohabitation and in restraint. How deep in the forest can human beings live and still maintain the trees as well as ourselves? It is possible that this experiment is about what is really meant when people talk about living in harmony with nature: learning to sing the descant rather than the melody. Living in a park, being but one of many creatures, rearranges the score. You learn to listen for the other voices. You get excited when you hear them.

Years before I lived here I read a passage in a book by Abraham Joshua Heschel that has stayed with me: "The greatest hindrance to knowledge is our adjustment to conventional notions, to mental cliches. Wonder or radical amazement, the state of maladjustment to words and notions, is, therefore, a prerequisite for an authentic awareness of that which is." If I look at a mountain and think I know what a mountain is, I will see only what I already know, and what I know is not only limited, it may not be true. Seeing an otter, or watching a wild turkey saunter across the backyard, or hearing the antiphonal hooting of bears at night is the beginning of the wonder, the radical amazement that sustains me here.

I had always imagined myself settling along a rugged coast somewhere in New England or northern California. I would live in a house that stood on stilts above the water; the wind would be a constant companion. The surf would crash on the rocks below, the tides would plunder the beach. If there were mountains in this picture they were far off in the distance. They could have been clouds.

As it turned out, I moved inland, not because I knew already that I loved the forest, but because I loved someone who did. It must have something to do with love's transforming power that before long I had abandoned my ideal landscape for the one I see when I look out the window of this room: a sea of hemlock and pine, and the wind riffling it; water rushing down the creekbed; the saddle of the mountain that rests in this valley like a glacial erratic. That I can see these things—that is, that I can look at them and not know them and so begin to see them—might be because they were not in my head to begin with.

Outside my window the snow is falling hard and fast. And I think: there is no misery in the sound of the wind.

Reynolds Price

A Grounded Life

THIS WILL READ, at first glance, like an exercise in rapt narcissism. What I mean to offer instead is a seldom-made observation about the function of landscape, natural and manmade objects, and familiar spaces in our lengthening lives. At a deeper level, I suspect, my observation means to suggest one barely mentioned reason for the savage glee with which white Americans have leveled this country and its natural contents since their arrival five centuries ago. I'll state the observation as a principle. *A sane human being, as life proceeds, will value certain spots on the Earth—certain lakes, roads, rooms, individual trees—as abiding reminders of significant moments in his or her earlier life.* And the principle has a reversed mirror-face that most adults have glimpsed more than once. *Self-revulsion, self-hate, will keep a creature moving in the hope of avoiding—if not entirely shedding—precisely grounded memories inherent in certain scenes, certain views, or the contents of rooms he or she has poisoned with large or trivial vicious acts and gestures and words.* Hence, in part at least, our notorious restlessness—far more destructively fugitive in recent centuries than Attila and his horsemen—as we've hauled ourselves and our hapless kin from state to state in the futile hope of abandoning personal failure and the stench it deposits on houses, streets, lawns.

The plural pronouns in that last sentence are deceitful on my part, for one of the odd things about my life as a twentieth-century middle-class white American adult has been my groundedness. Granted, my childhood was gypsy—my parents and I moved restlessly about in eastern and central North Carolina through the thirties; then joined by my one brother in 1941, we continued to wander until—when I was fourteen—we settled at last in the capital, Raleigh (by then I'd lived in thirteen houses, or sets of rooms, in six small towns).

At the age of eighteen I went a short twenty-two miles northwest to Duke University in Durham; and with the exception of four years at Oxford University in the fifties and early sixties, I've lived there ever since. Only last month I marked, with relief and no small pride, my thirtieth anniversary in a house I own by a small country pond in the edge of dense woods. It's a powerful hope—no guarantee of course—that the rest of my life will reel itself out here in these

bright rooms with views onto blue herons, deer, coons, bea-
vers, snakes (lethal and harmless), huge snapping turtles, swift
plucky kingfishers, squirrels, hawks, crows, doves, a thousand
more creatures, plus the mainly benign spoiled pet-dogs of
neighbors, and their patient brutal cats.

I can sit on a porch on the east of my house, on a clement
day, and watch not merely the day's representatives of rare and
wild life but also as many sites of private memory on the yard,
around the water's edge, and into the woods as that day's
memory discovers for me. I came to this piece of Carolina
woods when I was twenty-five years old (I lived in a nearby
trailer before buying my present house); and with thirty-seven
years of residence behind me, I can find at will and savor or regret the only barely invisible shapes of my remembered body
as it moved through acts of mute and tranquil contemplation,
melancholia and fear, laughable failure, and all but unimaginable love.

To take two examples—I've never shared the American
male obsession with the automobile. Cars for me, even before
they'd clearly become the curse of the Earth, were only conve-
niences, means for unavoidable movement. But in the early
years of my publishing career, I grew a little cash-proud and
owned a twenty-year series of Mercedeses. My first one was
maddeningly delicate, sure to be mysteriously uncrankable
on any damp morning, and I became a fairly adept jump-
starter of its engine. One cold morning, though, as I stood by
the open passenger door and gave the car a firm push down-

hill, a farcical mishap ensued. The wheels began to roll, I leapt into the driver's seat, slammed the door, and readied myself to pop the engine. Then in an instant I made a hard discovery—the steering wheel was locked in position, the wheels were locked in a hard-left direction, straight down a steep rocky hill to a creek in winter flood. I frantically pumped the brake—dead too—so as my downhill plunge gained speed, I saw I was aimed for a favorite handsome beech tree, and I braced myself for the fated collision. It occurred; in a moment I realized that I'd received no serious physical damage, though the car's front end and underbody transmission were considerably less well off. Imagine the ignominy of phoning your car-insurer and confessing that you've just suffered a major collision in your front yard. More than twenty years later, though, I and the struck beech tree are thriving; but a solid scar on its trunk reminds me often of a riotous moment and one more rescue from serious harm.

Another site—on the green hill behind my study—summons for me, many times a year, a tragic event from nearly three decades ago: the assassination of Martin Luther King, Jr. A friend and I had finished dinner that night in April 1968 when I switched on the TV for a glimpse of the news; there was the fresh addition to America's dreadful toll, the blight that rode us so hard in that decade. In complete silence my friend and I walked out the back door, up the path to the hill, and lay on our backs on thick warm pasture grass. Overhead was only the sky; and in the country, without the competition of city glare, the usual zillion stars were burning cold as ever. I recall we stayed there for more than an hour—still barely speaking, adrift in whatever private balked thoughts—before it felt even halfway safe to enter the house again with its man-made light.

Again, in the years I've staked out a life on the same hill's downside, I've bonded a crowd of other memories to individual spots on the ground, in the trees above, even to separate pieces of furniture, marks on the wall. Many of them are of a happily untellable nature, moments or days from the past when my own mind and body broke through to another's with an intimate daring that's at least as rewarding as all my glad hours of solitude.

The old fact then may seem a small, even an oddly skewed pleasure, but I'm powerfully convinced that no one who's moved with the harried frequency of so many of my fellow citizens can begin to think his or her way into the deep contentment and firm grounding of a longterm squatter. I'm proud to have been one and trust to continue, eventually maybe in the form of my ashes.

Nancy Lord

A Crying Country

SUMMERS, I LIVE in a cabin on a rocky Alaskan beach, separated by an inlet of fast water and tidal rips from the nearest accumulations of people. Ostensibly, I live here to fish, to earn a living catching and selling salmon. The truth is, fishing is just an excuse.

I love the beach where we fish—the fresh look of the shoreline after every tide, the volcanic peak that rises from the fog, eagles winging past, bears that walk the tideline at night, always the sound of the ocean moving in or out. I love the old, worn, ground-down-by-ice log posts that appear only at the lowest tides and mark where people, long before us, used to anchor their fishing nets. I love collecting agates and perfect round rocks from the beach and occasionally a piece of sea-polished glass.

I also love to leave the beach and hike up the creek to the top of the bluff and beyond, into forest and berry patch, around beaver ponds and across a lake by creaky rowboat. This is country where no one lives, no one comes to stay. Old moss-hung trees fall and no one hears them. Trails are flattened by the drag of beaver tails. Spiders string webs, and moose leave catches of stiff hairs among the alders. Trout jump, and jump, and jump.

On a morning late in May, Ken and I hike up the creek and into the woods. This time of year, with the ferns just unfurling, the devil's club only beginning to leaf on its cudgel end, it's possible as it never is later in the summer to move through the country, to see it almost bare. We circle the beaver pond that's expanded to flood our trail, climb over downed trees. Salmonberry are already in bloom, pink petals wide and silk-smooth. Here and there, last summer's highbush cranberries are still hanging on, reduced to wrinkled red shells. We hike and row and hike some more, toward mountains draped with clouds.

We find, this day, what we've come to see. The pit is deep, a depression in the ground, perhaps four feet lower than the forest floor. It's not the depth that's so remarkable, but the exact rectangular shape, the outline of two rooms. One is perhaps fifteen by twenty feet, the other a third that size. Rimmed with ridges of earth, they're pined with a break in the wall between them. Another break opens the large room to the outside.

I've been here once before, but I'm still taken by surprise, still overcome by something I can't easily explain. I want to hold my breath, stop time, go back. *People lived here.* The pit is all that remains of a traditional Dena'ina Indian house—a *barabara,* as they were called by the Russians. A winter house, dug into the ground but then framed with short walls of posts and logs, surrounded with sod, a roof of overlapping sheets of birch bark or animal hides.

It was a long time ago, and it wasn't. It was before Captain Cook sailed by in 1778, before epidemics of smallpox, measles, whooping cough, flu, and tuberculosis wiped out entire villages. It was not so long ago that the country's forgotten. The land holds the memory in ridges of earth, in deep holes, in the cry of a jay and the smell of softened pitch. A wall. A doorway. How many feet walked through? How many stories were told?

A spruce tree—one of the largest in the area—grows from one corner of the main room; another, somewhat smaller, stands in the pit itself. Either must be at least a couple of hundred years old.

Dena'ina, today, live in a village north of here, in houses built from milled lumber. Most work as commercial fishermen and hold on to many of the old ways. Another village, not far down the coast, was abandoned only in the late 1920s when its remaining people decided to join the larger community to the north. Other Dena'ina have disappeared into other cities and towns, into the prevailing culture.

I try to see this pit as a full barabara, in snow, smoke curling from the hole in the roof, snowshoe trails beaten around it. Behind it, I position a cache built off the ground, on peeled poles, filled with bales of dried salmon. I imagine the smell of boiling meat, sounds of people talking, babies. Winter was a time of rest. January is known, in Dena'ina, as The Month We Sing.

Right now, King Salmon Month, this barabara would be silent, empty, the country's new grass closing in around it. The people would be on the beach below, camped, feasting on fresh salmon, splitting and hanging salmon to dry in the smoke of an alder fire, beginning again the cycle of preservation that would see them through another winter.

Summers on the beach, we catch salmon to sell to Japan. We eat a few, hang some in our smokehouse. In The Month Leaves Turn Yellow, we leave the beach, not to this country above, but to a country away, a house in a city.

We walk around the pit, farther into the woods. Everywhere, I think I see unnatural depressions, two walls forming a right angle. I know pits are here and I can't see them exactly, or what I see are only dead trees fallen and rotted, covered with moss. I know there must be more than one house to the village. We pick our way through brush, over more deadfall. We step to the rim of another pit: deeper than the first, smaller, two rectangular rooms of different sizes connected with a pass in the wall between, unmistakable.

A mountain shoulder we can see from our camp is known to the Dena'ina as Ridge Where We Cry. Shem Pete, one of the oldest living Dena'ina, spoke about that place a few years ago: "They would sit down there. Everything is in view. They can see their whole country. Everything is just right under them. They think about their brothers and their fathers and mothers. They remember that, and they just sit down there and cry. That's the place we cry all the time, 'cause everything just show up plain."

Those of us who come here only as visitors will never know what it is to truly live here, to be a part of this place. Ken and I, who moved to Alaska as adults, can never know the feeling of looking at this land and wanting to cry—not at how beautiful the untamed country is or how mysterious what we find in it—but for our brothers and fathers and mothers, our history and our place where "everything show up plain."

Bunchberry flowers, four-lobed sets of perfect white, stretch from the hollow of a decayed log. From somewhere in the trees floats the *sweet-sweet-sweet* of a sparrow. This is a place more wild today than it's been, probably, for most of the last millennium—since the Dena'ina first came through the mountains.

Despite all its natural beauty, I feel the loss, the absence, the missing continuum. I love this place, but I'm starting almost from scratch, trying to see not only what is wild but what belongs to people. I'm trying, with what I know and what I imagine, to begin again with story.

Cathy Johnson

River and Rock

I WAS BORN in these Missouri hills, and since then I have migrated only twenty-eight miles, from the gentle inclines of Independence to the steep, glacier-formed landscape north of the Missouri River. That slight change in compass bearing allows me to see my country with fresh eyes, to search for northern lights, to feel a different pull along the veins of my arms. When I was a child, to take a midnight ride north of the river was to find the exotic close to home. It still is.

The fact that I continue to live in the northwest quadrant of Missouri grounds me in a broader landscape, but one of intimate resonances; I know this country. I am both at home here and aware of change in a way I could never be in less familiar territory. I watch for signs of dis-ease like a worried mother, and find an ancestral and atavistic comfort in the natural, the cyclical, the anticipated. The Cherokee word for land also encompasses history, culture, and spirituality; it's my definition as well. Rootedness has more to do with imagination and commitment than with complacency, and it is history—my own, my family's, the Earth's—that holds me.

Time is measured here in the syncopated chant of chorus frogs, in the call of male redwing blackbirds, in a bobcat's midnight scream. In the seasonal thunder of goose-wing on the Mississippi Flyway, and the silent procession of wildflowers. In the scent of January's thaw, redolent as a fresh-opened tin of Chinese tea. In the phases of the moon, in the rock beneath my feet, in the long-running show that is the Missouri River.

The river flows through my imagination; it has made its indelible channel there as well as on the land, where you can still trace the complex braidings of the ancient riverbed. Peketanoui—river of the big canoes—holds the moon in its swath, cradling it in a sheet of silver light. It bores through layers of limestone and silt, and though temporarily tethered by the locks and dams of the Army Corps of Engineers, it patiently, inexorably fulfills its own agenda. Unlike dams, rivers are made for the long haul.

Huge catfish scour the river bottom in search of food, their sensitive, whiskerlike barbels of more use than eyes in the silty murk. Blue cats upward of three hundred pounds were caught here a century ago; a 100-pound fish is not uncommon today. Herons stalk the shallows, startling the air with pterodactyl croaks. While musseling is legal in only three areas, broad beds tempt shell-rustlers to go their outlaw ways.

I damn their greed, yet understand their motivation. In a limestone draw just down from my place are the jackstraw remains of a moonshiner's cabin. My father may have gone there in the deep of night in his efforts to carry the family through the Great Depression. I'm told he ran booze in the trunk of his car when this area was wilder than it is today.

My grandmother's maiden name was Clark, and family legend has it that it came directly from William Clark, of Lewis and Clark fame. I was never moved to study the two explorers until I learned that both men were also naturalists. The fact that I do the same work makes me smile, as does reading their accounts of a river bend not ten minutes from where I write. I sketch a fish and compare my drawing to Clark's, looking for the family resemblance.

It's the rock as well as the river that keeps me. Pale outcroppings of Pennsylvanian-era limestone poke through the soil. Three hundred million years old, it has much to tell the paleobiologist: a certain forensic knowledge extrapolates a tale of life and death at the bottom of a shallow inland sea when this area was equatorial. I don't have to move—the landscape's done it for me.

Small marine animals—ammonites, brachiopods, corals —stud the stone matrix. Bug-eyed trilobites stare, blind and noncommittal, from the rock. As water levels fluctuated, bits of plant life were also fossilized, flat as the flowers pressed between the pages of my grandmother's yellowing field guide. My mother drew these fossils as I do today. Stone that was once alive has a power in the mind. Animal, vegetable, or mineral? Here, there's no easy answer.

Not far from my cabin is a ledge of rock, scimitar shaped, where Native Americans found shelter on the long hunts up from the river. I touch prehistoric smoke stains on the roof and half expect to find soot on my fingertips; I look for stone tools beneath the ledge. The limestone is rich in flint; at nearby Nebo Hill, Stone Age people flourished from 7000 to 5000 B.C., and I find evidence of the everyday washed up in my creek.

There is no stream at the ledge, only the patient, meticulous sculpting of snowmelt and rain, but someday this shallow cave of permeable stone will retreat into the hillside and disappear. It won't be soon.

Fifteen thousand years ago, the glacier that gave birth to the river began to recede. Meltwater deposited new, unfamiliar rocks. Entombed in ice, rocks and boulders moved too, scribing the bedrock with long arrows pointing north; the hitchhikers were jettisoned here like excess baggage along the Oregon Trail. Such glacial erratics are common north of the Missouri, marking the apogee of ice. Native Americans used the largest of these quartzite monoliths as landmarks and ceremonial sites. A smaller version sits on my cabin's deck, marking land of my own, though my ceremony is solitary and cerebral.

As geology forms this land, it informs it with a sense of continuity on a grand scale. An odd enough reason to stay, but one of the best I can offer. That, and the river that moves through, pointing to the past and the possibility of moonshine.

John Daniel

Turnings of Seasons

I MUST HAVE been thirteen or so when I announced to my parents that I would attend the University of Oregon and study forestry. I had never been to the Northwest —we lived in a suburb of Washington, D.C.—but I had been reading Bernard DeVoto's books on the opening of the West. I knew that Oregon, which then I must have pronounced ARE-uh-GAHN, had to be the best and wildest place on Earth.

I got it wrong and I got it right. In 1966 I did indeed steer the rattling Jeep my mother had given me across the country to the great state of my imagining. Not to the U of O, however, but to Reed College in Portland. And not to study forestry—not to study much of anything, it turned out, in part because LSD arrived in Oregon the same year I did. Things got very clear and very confusing.

I dropped out of Reed and spent the late sixties on the move, mostly between Portland and San Francisco, changing jobs, homes, and preoccupations at a pace I now marvel at. My attention was focused inward then—I was spellbound by my own epiphanies and chronic perplexities. The great Northwest, for all I saw of it, was rain and mist, green fields and fronts of forest sliding through the frame of a car window.

Then once, hitching north to Portland, a friend and I were stranded at midnight on Interstate 5 in northern California. It was clear and brutally cold, the freeway almost deserted. The moonlit cliffs of Castle Crags stood west of us, and above us to the north loomed the snowy ghost of Mount Shasta. We stamped our feet, hunching against the cold, and somehow our misery made moon and crags and mountain more intensely beautiful. There was glory and solemnity everywhere. That night, for the first time, I was in the presence of the western land. We shivered there for hours before a long-haul trucker took pity on us and drove us clear to Portland.

Not long after that I was climbing mountains. To a kid whose wildest expeditions had involved a few miles of the Appalachian Trail, the Cascade volcanoes were sheer exultation. I remember my first climb of Mount Hood, standing at ten thousand feet with fat stars glowing as I had never seen them, the land spreading wide with its specks of human light, the sovereign radiance of dawn under way in the east. It all made a cosmos lit with possibility. I watched a spider climbing the crusted snow and felt certain that both of us, so different and so wildly out of place, were doing just what we were born to do.

For several years I climbed with little skill but hungrily, as if crags and clouds and glacial brilliance were a secret language I was always on the verge of understanding. I sensed obscurely that the riddle of the mountains somehow was the riddle of my life, that in the wild hills if anywhere I might discover the sure and undivided self I wanted to be. There were moments when I found it. On Mount Olympus in Washington, for instance—the twenty-mile hike from the Hoh rainforest had been a kind of purgatory, and as windy vapors obscured and revealed the knifey ridges around me, I lay still as stone on the summit pinnacle, wanting nothing that was not there.

I worked in the mountains, too. For parts of two years, within sight of Mount St. Helens, I helped the Weyerhaeuser Timber Company strip its land of trees. Setting chokers on a high-lead side was the hardest job of my life, but it was exciting in its violence, and it was educational. Seeing old-growth forest reduced to raw slopes and muddy streams occasioned the first twinges of an ecological conscience, yet at the same time I learned to respect the men I worked with. They bore up with spirit under wearing and dangerous labor, they wore their lives like comfortable clothing, and they knew the land far better than I did as a weekend climber. Riding the jolting crummie out of the woods at the end of the day, I would doze off to their easy talk of elk and salmon, rebuilding engines, splitting cedar shakes.

I drifted into the seventies, still majoring in self-doubt and confusion. That I belonged in the West was all I knew for sure. I lived with friends in San Francisco, dabbled in Zen meditation, climbed in Yosemite, protested the war, took drugs and sporadic college courses. Nothing I did seemed to fit with anything else. It was a ramshackle life and not at all clear who was living it. I had felt since childhood that maybe I could write, but the few lines I was able to force out seemed merely contemptible. They confirmed what I'd known all along: I had nothing to write about.

I came back to Oregon in 1973 for a railroad job, and I came to a different country. My girlfriend and I awoke on a gray February morning at a highway rest area near Klamath Falls, just east of the Cascades. We looked around in puzzled disappointment. No tall Douglas firs, no rushing streams, no emerald fields, no green at all—just sagebrush flats and barren hills studded with a few disconsolate junipers. Somehow I'd missed the fact that two-thirds of Oregon is desert and steppe. I decided I wouldn't stay long in that bleak country.

I stayed ten years. The job, one of those for which the railroad is justly notorious, amounted to an extended fellowship in fooling around. I climbed and skied and fished in the Cascades, but I also explored the unfamiliar dry country. I found I liked how junipers apportioned themselves on the rocky slopes, each shaggy tree standing solitary and whole, and even clumps of sage and crusty scabrocks came to seem not bleak but beautiful. In all that spacious stillness, something opened inside me. I remember sitting on a rock one afternoon watching cloud shadows travel the hills, a light breeze stirring the bronco grass and the hair of my arms. I realized that beneath my twenty-five-year-old uncertainties I was whole and maybe even happy. The great dry land seemed an open secret, a secret with room for me.

It was there, in the Klamath Basin, that I began to write. I labored over clumsy and passionate short stories—Hemingway sorts of things about fathers and sons, coming of age, sitting in bars—until I noticed that the best passages had less to do with characters and plot than they did with landscape. It slowly came to me that I didn't want to create human worlds out of words. I wanted to touch with words the beauties and mysteries of nature, and so my fiction died, and poems and essays grew.

I quit the railroad after a few years and moved to a shack on a friend's ranch near Bonanza. I wrote about the dusty stones, the smell of sage in a summer storm, the electrifying cries of coyotes and the colloquies of great horned owls, the stalwart junipers transfigured into green flames as sundown flared the rimrock red. As I lived and wrote through a few turnings of seasons I began to know land in a new way, not as a weekend playground or a scenic view, but as a home I might somehow belong to, though none of it belonged to me.

I spent most of the eighties in California again, pursuing an invaluable writing apprenticeship at Stanford University. (At last, in my mid-thirties, I had a good reason to go to college.) But leaving Oregon had felt like leaving home, and when my wife and I returned in 1988, we came to stay. We lived six years in Portland, where the work was, but that good gray city of taverns and bookstores wasn't our place. In cities, even the best ones, I always feel like a guest. The party goes on, the partiers are mostly friendly, but eventually I tire of all the noise and people. I want to go home.

Our chance came last year, and we bolted to the country —to a plain brown box of a house on an acre of Douglas firs and blackberry thickets in the Coast Range foothills near Eugene. We traded streetlights for stars, Portland's sirens and traffic roar for wind in the trees, frogs and owls, the seasonal music of a little stream that we call Winter Creek. It's taken forty-six years and thirty-two dwellings in a dozen states, but I think I've arrived where I want to be.

It could have been somewhere else. Once a place draws roots from you, as the Klamath Basin drew them from me, you can probably put them down in many kinds of soil. But I'm glad it's here, in the country and climate I came to as a college freshman, my entire life ahead of me, excited as a young explorer entering a New World. I feel the same way now. I'm eager to watch the changing light, through the day and through the seasons, in the grove of mossy-sided trees behind the house. I've started to clear a garden in the brambles. I want to watch the cherry trees we planted extend their limbs and rise, and in my mind I want to watch their roots go deep and wide.

I've lived a life of moving on, chasing possibility from place to place. Now I'm ready for greater travels. I'm ready to journey into home.

I haven't lost my love for mountains, though I don't climb much anymore—I hike between them and around them. And neither have I lost the taste for drier land I learned in eastern Oregon. I travel there and to farther places, to Baja and Death Valley, the canyon country of the Four Corners. I go for space and stillness, to know my wholeness by the clarity of stone and sky. Then home again, to the easy and insistent rain that falls here like a benediction, dripping from the Douglas firs, jostling trilliums and rhododendrons, dancing on the roof and gurgling softly in the downspouts, entering that darkness from which mushrooms rise, ferns unfurl, and even words sometimes will find their way.

.

M. Garrett Bauman

Moon Walking

FEBRUARY 9, 1993. Two degrees Fahrenheit. A mile from the nearest road on the western fringe of New York's Finger Lakes region. Elevation: 1,834 feet. Latitude: 42 degrees, 38 minutes; longitude: 77 degrees, 49.5 minutes.

I like the frozen crunch of fact under foot when I set out for a winter walk at midnight. With just a wedge of moon, I will walk for miles in the woods. If that seems intimidating, consider that Nunda, New York (where I live), orbits the sun at more than sixty-seven thousand miles per hour, and the Milky Way rockets through untracked space at speeds we cannot determine. All while we think we're well located at our lighted addresses. So when a winter itch creeps up the back of my legs,

I know it's time to walk in the dark. If I wait until spring, I won't be within millions of miles of where I am now.

Two days of snow and ripping winds have dragged drifts into hollows and rippled dune patterns across the field. Tonight the wind died and the moon shines. The porch steps crack under my weight like branches splitting in an ice storm. The sound echoes from the woods.

Cold assaults my nostrils—the ether cold of windless night that radiates heat into space. My body heat drains through sweater and coat. My ears know where the pores in my knitted hat are. On a night like this I realize how cold the universe is, how few are those 100 billion nuclear candles that warm our galaxy. Twenty times as many cells warm each of us.

The pore between our sun and the nearest star is 25 trillion miles wide. Into that gap radiates heat from maple buds, crevices of car engines run hours ago, steam in kitchens, and the fluffed-out owl. Simple physics—heat moves to cold. If all life, all stars, all fuel were consumed in supernovas—if we spread all known heat like butter over the cold platter of the universe—could it warm space's absolute zero by even one degree?

Maybe it is the fear of being absorbed by such cold that keeps us indoors on winter nights. Yet most people can walk more securely in the dark than they suspect. With the moon and reflective snow cover, I can see the red barn and brown grass across the valley. Deer, rabbit, and turkey prints show clearly. Tonight's brilliant moon flies above scattered hazy clouds. The landscape glows in a pale, watery luminescence. Moonlight should be cold; yet when I step from the shadows, the light feels warm. I may be kidding myself, of course. It's not much, just a sigh, a dream of heat from the cold sky. The dry, fluffy snow squeaks with each step, and the flakes glitter, so it feels as though I'm walking through a field of stars; thousands of them sparkle in the flakes underfoot.

Walking in the night reminds me of an elderly woman named Eva who lived in my house when I was a child. She had been blind for twenty years, and often didn't know her stockings sagged like an elephant's skin around her ankles. But she taught me to read and to identify birds from an old encyclopedia. I still recall the glossy pages with the lush birds, even though the years have closed over her and that lost book—"Describe it to me," she'd say. And when I did, she might say, "Ah, that's an oriole," and have me read the name under it. I'd stare at the flaming orange-and-black bird and then at the glint of light in her dead eyes. So we felt our way toward sight, each a moon for the other's midnight.

I head for the gully trail, dropping two hundred feet in a quarter mile. As I move under tree shadows, the stars at my feet disappear. My teeth and lungs sting. I spot fresh prints in the snow and recall stories of bobcats ambushing deer from under trees. Branches hang thickly over me, and I hope the bobcat sees well and lacks ambition. At the bottom, the creek is stiffening into ice, gurgling halfheartedly as it grinds to a halt. Rocks that are awash wear slick caps of ice. Here at the farthest edge of my property, I mark my territory, a pathetic wisp of steam vanishing upward. On the way back, thighs, ears, and cheeks pay for walking in the dark. My body has begun shutting off its heat hoard to save brain and heart.

The cold-cracking tree limbs sound as if they could start a split through the earth, as though the brittle air could shatter like glass. As I pass the frozen pond, I spot the goose that camps on our property—white feathers against the white, snowed-over pond. She stands on one leg, silent, waiting for water. A yellow light from the house blinks through the trees, and the cold moon glows above. The bass lie on the bottom of the pond, the ice above them inching down. What would we do if the darkness and cold should really take hold? I slap my numb thighs and tramp home.

Lynne Bama

The Unseen Mountain

I FELL IN LOVE with Wyoming twenty-six years ago, on my first day in the state, right on this spot. Here among the ranks of mountains east of Yellowstone Park I saw a range of hills capped by a sandstone outcrop where ancient limber pines clawed at the stillness. Out beyond it, to the south, the land opened into a great bowl on whose far side rose forested slopes through which the reddish tints of old lavas sullenly glowed. On that day, as now, the whole panorama was enclosed by a lid of overcast.

I had climbed the ridge intently, concentrating on my footing. Only when I got to the top did I turn around and discover that the clouds on the other side of the valley had blown away. What had seemed to be a complete landscape had miraculously enlarged, and I found myself staring at an enormous volcanic rampart, its face streaked and marbled with veins of new-fallen snow.

I sat down on a rock, stunned by this unexpected, looming presence, by the eerie combination of nearness and deep space and silence. In that moment the shape of my life changed. Two years later I moved to Wyoming and have since lived nowhere else.

One of the first things I learned here was that my preconceptions of "The West" didn't fit. Like many newcomers to the Equality State, I arrived on the broad interstate of cliché, expecting to find a country filled with Stetsoned figures on horseback. Such canned images—the stock-in-trade of chambers of commerce and tourist commissions—have their uses, giving the casual visitor a ready-made package of concepts, a list of places to go and things to do. But after I had lived here awhile I began to see them for what they are—not responses to the terrain itself but merely efficient methods of managing large numbers of people. Lately I've come to suspect that the endurance of the cowboy myth is based less on his personal qualities than on those of the scenery around him.

I noticed, too, that the stereotypes that have been nurtured in this country have demanded a certain amount of cut-and-fill. They have left a scar. The cowboy culture that so many of us romanticize was built on a tragic and foredoomed confrontation with nature, the struggle between man and wildness that is symbolized on Wyoming license plates by the cowboy on the bucking bronco. Although the *High Noon* glamor of its self-reliant heroes still draws the discontented and unfulfilled from every quarter, the mystique of the West has left a legacy of erosion, overgrazed ranges, and diminished wildlife.

As I wait for the clouds to blow off the mountain and bring back that moment from years ago, I find that the gulf that impresses me today is not in the land in front of me, but in myself, in the difference between what I knew then and what I know now. To arrive at a real understanding of this region I had to leave the highways, and even the dirt roads, and find a footpath to a spot like this.

On that first day here I knew so little. I might have recognized Indian paintbrush, but crazyweed, pussytoe, squawbush, Rocky Mountain juniper, and limber pine were strangers. I did not see how these hills had been shaped by a century of livestock grazing. Nor did I know the native plants that had died out as a result, to be replaced with new ones come, like myself, to put down their alien roots into this thin and stony soil. All I could see at first was abundance—the bighorn sheep and pronghorn antelope, the great herds of deer on the meadows at dawn, the tracks of black bear in the forest. I did not feel the absence of the wolves and bison that had vanished, could not miss what I had never known.

The pine trees around me reach maturity after two or three hundred years. They were surely standing on this spot when the first whites came into the country with their traps and guns, their cattle and wagons. Those trunks that have fallen, their scabby, furrowed bark preserved by the dry air, must once have cast their shade on the original peoples, tribes forgotten by history, who lived on pine nuts and grass seeds and bighorn mutton. Once when I was walking on a footpath near my house I found a tiny arrowhead made of red chert poking out of the soil. An archaeologist friend told me it had been broken and mended, too precious to discard. I still have it on my desk, to remind me that those who lasted longest here left the least evidence. Sometimes I wonder what mark I will leave here myself—the grasses I have let grow around the house, a few crumbling foundation walls in the sage. Or will my legacy be an absence—a vanished flower or silenced bird?

I've been up here on the ridgetop for several hours now, and the clouds are still in place. The mountain, I see, is not going to repeat its magic act of years ago. But it doesn't have to, for now I know it's there.

David Guterson

Surrounded by Water

I LIVE ON AN island in Puget Sound that inspires the
envy and loathing of mainlanders. The envy, I suppose,
grows out of the delusion that islanders live an idyllic existence; the loathing grows out of the corollary delusion that
islanders have retreated from mainland affairs, fled from the
intractable problems of our time, taken refuge from the late
twentieth century on a pleasant curve of sunlit beach. The
envy and the loathing eventually run together until they are
no longer mirror images of one another but rather a tangled
web of emotion that prevents clarity about island living. In
this way, islands remain ideas instead of places in the hearts
and minds of certain mainlanders.

These people, ironically, own a kind of truth, since an island *is* in large part an idea, a place we invent for our own peculiar purposes and according to our personal requirements. After all, what makes an island truly an island other than that we call it such? The standard definition—*surrounded by water*—can be applied to whole countries and continents and to the sandbars in the ends of nameless creeks and to the rocks appearing at low tide. The point here is not merely semantic but rather a matter of perception. Arriving on an island by boat or bridge we are offered no clue to its status as an island or to how it is divorced from the mainland. Instead we perceive it as an island by intention; it is something we conjure inwardly. We exert ourselves to feel the full sweep of surrounding waters even when we are out of sight of the sea, even where the shore does nothing to suggest that it bends infinitely onward.

Islands are as much imagined as real and live in the mind's eye with as much raw power as they live in the world of tides and winds. They are thus, and variously, places of danger, places of retreat, holy places, prisons, the sanctuaries of the rich, haunts of castaways, hermits, and saints, bastions of commerce, piracy and trade, bedrock of forts, monasteries and mansions and cradles of lost civilizations. We conjure islands according to our lights and with no small measure of drama, too—*Robinson Crusoe,* Napoleon in exile, Alcatraz, the sway of palms. The susurrus of trade winds, the light on Ibiza, the whitewashed facades of Mykonos, the locus of long interred treasure. We take our honeymoons on the easy isles, we seek the smell of orchids there, we imagine ourselves all sleek and brown and reborn as younger people. Carrying a sixth sense for islands in the mind, we transform and inspire their landscapes, gilding them with a poignant light and painting the stones that litter their beaches in the heightened colors of romance.

Islands fill mainlanders with an unabashed yearning for a life simpler than the one they endure, a pared-down life in which all that is elemental—sea, wind, sun, love, the last light of day, the sand beneath fingernails—is brought to the forefront of existence. Islands are also paradoxical places: they simultaneously liberate and confine. For every island like Patos in the nearby San Juans—a place to urge one's soul toward the sublime—there is another like McNeil just west of Tacoma, home to a federal penitentiary. These two extremes contain one another—the moat of water that keeps others out also keeps islanders in. The moat of water that makes an islander feel secure also makes an islander a prisoner.

Bainbridge Island, where I have lived for ten years, is intimately connected to Seattle by ferry and to the mainland westward by the Agate Pass Bridge, but these facts have not prevented its citizens from developing island psyches. We know ourselves trapped and emancipated, and our view of ourselves and of the surrounding world is transformed when we cross the water. On the mainland we experience that intimation of a continent rolling hugely and relentlessly toward us—tossing the misery of the world at our heads—whereas at home we feel a countervailing certainty that the nation's travail, so distantly troubling, can never reach us across the water. In return for this delusion of safety, we islanders trade in the larger world with all of its reckless beauty. Abroad and about in the mainland universe, we are at best thrill-seekers or tourists.

Islands are limited by surrounding waters, which impose on islanders certain duties and conditions foreign to any mainlander. An error in behavior—belligerence at a school board meeting, say, or a strident comment made in passing—is irredeemable. A lapse in judgment while parking one's car, an impolitic recklessness with a shopping cart, impatience with the service at an island restaurant, or heated yelling at the auto mechanic longtime islanders are enamored of—these things mark and define an islander indelibly as not belonging. One learns to step lightly, to be on time to anything formal and late for anything informal, to apologize and praise profusely and often—one learns to err on the side of caution in all of one's affairs. It is best to smile, to make gracious small talk, to be patient when there is no good reason to be. One never knows who is watching and judging, or cataloging all one's shortcomings.

Islanders are required, by the very nature of their landscape, to watch their step moment by moment. A simple conversation with a Little League coach about one's child's position in the batting order can be fraught with dark implications. A conversation in the ticket line at the theater can readily suggest the tide of ill-will that ebbs and flows over island affairs so endlessly and egregiously. No one treads easily on the emotions of another where the sea licks everywhere against an endless shoreline. Why take the chance that running roughshod with one's opinions might spoil everything? In this, of course, islands are like other places, but with a special difference that ups the ante: on an island there is no blending into an anonymous background, no neighboring community to shift toward. There is, instead, only water.

An enemy on an island, as in a prison, is an enemy forever and deeply. One result is that islanders take special pains to avoid the risks of engagement; another is a certain inbreeding of the spirit, too much held in, regret and silent brooding, a world whose inhabitants walk in trepidation, in fear of opening up. Considered and considerate, formal at every turn, we islanders are shut out from the deep interplay of minds, though adept at island gossip. We cannot speak freely because we are cornered: everywhere we turn there is water and more water, a limitless expanse in which to drown. We hold our breath and walk with care and this makes us who we are inside, constricted and reserved good neighbors.

On Bainbridge a trip to the grocery store can be the seminal event of the week. Like people in small places everywhere, we know or recognize everybody, and know how to place them in the hierarchy of islanders, for there is no privacy in paradise. She with the sixteen cans of stewed tomatoes is a part of the cabal of island thespians who live to perform before the rest of us; he with the frozen shrimp in his cart is divorced, unhappy, and part of a men's group that sometimes beats drums in the forest. Here is that man who could not contain himself last month at a baseball game played by nine-year-olds; here is the woman who lost her left breast, the accountant who lives alone on his boat, the keeper of horses, the dentist's first wife, the woman who enticed the dentist. Over there, sorting through lettuces, is the man of twenty-seven who was senior class president but has since disappointed all of us; and here is the mother of a forgotten quarterback, who reports enthusiastically that the former star is carrying a 3.6 at Stanford. That man in the loud tie led the charge last year against the monstrous apparition of a storm drain surtax: see how he buys expensive frozen dinners and is perennially in a hurry? This one is for saving the remaining farms and for more decorations in town at Christmas; that one has opined in the pages of our newspaper that our island has too many lawyers. The curmudgeon, the crank, the troublemaker, the philanderer, the girl who has been pregnant twice. How laughable that islands seem to mainlanders like places to get away from it all. If you want that sort of freedom from social torment, by all means stay on the mainland.

Outsiders sense none of these nightmarish matters and while ignorant of the island psychodynamic must nevertheless contend with our reluctance to let them move among us at all. Islands betray at every turn the zealousness of their citizens, who jealously guard the placement of stones and turn bilious through the height of the tourist season. Even on Bainbridge, a suburb of Seattle, we know this islander's disturbance in the psyche: mainlanders can visit, but they can't comprehend, so let them picnic or meander on bicycles: the ferry will eventually take them away, and they will leave behind only money. Our posture is neither an intellectual proposition or a conscious effort to deny entry to the castle; it is instead a frail human emotion bred and nurtured by a selfish love.

If an island is to mainlanders the dream of escape, it is to an islander a more complicated terrain: a miniature planet on which the force of surrounding waves keeps everyone bound to their place.

To my friends and acquaintances from other places—New York, Chicago, Los Angeles—who have visited me here over the years, Bainbridge Island seems much like a paradise. At any rate they have averred as much while standing on my porch looking out across the trees and have articulated their desire to live here too, freed from all of life's concerns.

Yet there is no island anywhere far enough offshore where one escapes from the human condition. And it is also true that no man is an island, sufficient unto himself and therefore immune to the bald facts of existence. The bell tolls for me as it tolls for you and can be heard even here, across the water. And because I hear it on the easy isle I can't delude myself, as others in other places might, that in moving elsewhere—to an island perhaps—I might be reborn in paradise.

In the electronic mecca of our imminent future, islands

will be more accessible places, and with the advent of the fax modem and the Home Shopping Channel, more people will opt to live on them. They will come in droves, like pioneers, doubtful at first as to the shape of their own souls, uncertain if they are indeed well-disposed to the vagaries of island living. It will gradually emerge that some feel claustrophobic—that the insular nature of island living feels like a claw that means to drown them. Others will experience that alteration of the spirit that inevitably shapes them into islanders—they will inwardly draw the boundaries of the place and incorporate them as their own. Within these boundaries their lives will feel truncated and small and secure and yet unbounded, and if they allow themselves this sort of indulgence their lives will feel romantic, too.

In a universe that is infinite and incomprehensible—in a world that is increasingly beyond all control—islands offer definition. They are every bit a fool's sort of paradise, and at the same time an antidote to reality. I live on mine with considerably mixed feelings, for Bainbridge is a society of prisoners who have chosen exile together. It is also a place whose limiting waters inspire the illusion of a finite order—a place, in short, for the best in humanity. An island is, like Earth itself, a small promise in an endless sea.

Alison Hawthorne Deming

Claiming the Yard

IME TO CUT back the overgrowth again. The pyracantha hedge has gone shapeless as uncombed hair. The paloverde has pressed a limb against the stucco chimney running up the east wall of my house. And the bougainvillea has sprawled beyond its capacity to hold its boughs upright. Even the aloes and agaves have sent satellite growths out from their roots, the outliers offending my idea of symmetry in the semicircular garden by the front door. The profusion always surprises me, though I have had three years to get used to desert living. When I'm not cutting back and pulling up, I'm struggling to keep plants alive that don't belong here—peppermint, petunias, tomatoes, and marigolds. Since the temperature in Tucson has been above 100 degrees for most of the past four months, my attempts at gardening look pretty crisp these days. I have mastered only clove-scented basil. *My basil trees,* I call them. The cluster of glistening sweetness thriving for six months in the backyard shade has grown three feet tall, sporting woody stalks an inch thick and leaves big as serving spoons. I don't have the heart to whack them down to make pesto.

My friends who know my dreamy penchant for oceans and woods find it strange that I live in the sun-beaten starkland of the Sonoran desert. To be honest, so do I. At times I feel green-deprived and would not be surprised to learn that there exists a psychic malady that can be cured only by the visual ingestion of green wildness.

But I love not only nature's beauty; I love also her weirdness and pig-headed persistence against hostile conditions. And the desert is nothing if not weird and pig-headed. Consider the spadefoot toad that uses its namesake appendages to dig a home underground, lies there without breathing for months—even years in severe drought—absorbing oxygen through its skin, then emerges to feed and breed at the first music of raindrops hitting the soil. Consider the range of desert dwellers requiring venom in order to survive: gila monster, ten species of rattlesnake, coral snake, scorpion, centipede, tarantula, black widow, brown recluse, and a poisonous frog known to kill the dog that licks it. Consider the placid saguaro cactus, a cool, phallic, water cask that takes its sweet time growing—fifty years before it bothers making arms. Living here has been humbling, teaching me that I don't know much about nature after all, that I am no master even of the small domain of my yard.

A yard, anywhere, is an expression of one's relationship with nature, a curious border zone between the wild and the domestic where we invite nature to come close, but not too close. Nature does not belong in the house. We buy chemical products to keep our space clear of fungi, mold, bacilli, mites, and fleas. Plants can come inside, if they are content to live in pots. We seal basement windows and crawl spaces to keep out feral cats. And, when a crusty cockroach or lacy newt sneaks out of the drain into our kitchen sink, we are shocked at its lack of respect for the border we've drawn. The shaping and ordering of the yard is a warning to nature: here dwells human will.

In the desert the conscientious homeowner gives up on lawn, replacing it with gravel and a few pleasingly arrayed arid-land shrubs and trees—Sonoran bird of paradise, oleander, prickly pear, Joshua tree, Chilean mesquite. After the January rains, the gravel sprouts with mustard, wild onion grass, tumbleweed, penstemon, and globe mallow. Most of my neighbors use Rapid-Kill and Round-Up to keep the gravel bare, to provide a more attractive background for their shrubs. Gallon jugs of the stuff are sold at grocery and drug stores. In my first years I resorted to arduous biannual weed-pulling, but I have decided that this fall I will let the front yard go wild and see what comes up.

I am inspired to do so by my earlier experiment with Arizona lupines. I had been accustomed to lupines in the Northeast. They grow in manic meadows along the coast of Maine and New Brunswick—startling spires of peppery deep blue, fuchsia, white, and pink quilting the roadsides. Lupines in the Northeast are bigger and more sturdy than most wildflowers; in fact, they are a runaway garden variety, or, as the field guide calls them, "escapes."

Shortly after moving to Arizona, I made a road trip north from Tucson to Globe. It was April, and I had no idea what to expect from spring in the desert. My route made a gradual ascent from creosote and saguaro terrain to one of varied grasses. The shoulder lit up with the burgundy tassels of bromegrass, and then deep blue began to line both sides of the road, a linear bouquet that extended for fifty miles. Pulling off to identify the bloom, I was surprised to discover that they were lupines—smaller in stature, leaf, and flower size, their color more subdued, but morphologically identical to the eastern runaways. A few miles farther on, lupines blanketed entire hillsides and arroyos, the ground tinted as if a cloud shedding blue shadow had drifted over.

The bloom passed as quickly as a cloud. I returned two weeks later to gather seed, and the task was a challenge. Not only had the flowers faded, the plants were blown flat and empty by hot, dry winds. I collected what pods I could find and brought them home to scatter in my yard.

Last spring my captives bloomed out of the gravel by the mailbox. It was then, when that small, wild, blue meadow flared up and passed into dross, that I began to feel at home.

Gene Logsdon

Fields of Plenty

MY HOME GROUND appears to urban America as a dull, plain landscape inhabited by dull, plain people, which is precisely why my wife and I chose to move here twenty years ago. There are fewer than 24,000 people in the whole county, fewer than a hundred years ago. We could see nothing here that would tempt economic "development"; nothing to attract the tourist to violate our privacy; nothing to charm the media into turning us into lies. No breathtaking views of either mountain or valley lure the vacationer. No large body of water puts property taxes at the mercy of rich peoples' condos and second homes. No significant event by history book standards has occurred here; no one the least bit famous ever lived here. The landscape appears to be wall-to-wall corn bounded by thistles and poison ivy. We are saved by an accident of geography, the only armor that can effectively fend off greed. We live in Flyover Land and pray that it stays that way.

After nine years of being mashed in the crowds of train terminals, airports, and traffic jams until I felt like a maggot, we settled on the edge of the Corn Belt in north-central Ohio not only because we thought this rural community would remain relatively unspoiled, but because it was my homeland. Other communities might have worked just as well, but here I already had forty years of knowledge to build on. And I wanted, in my contrary fashion, to prove that a person could go home again—provided there is a homeland to go back to.

Returning to familiar ground, I knew that beneath the corn was a great treasure and natural wonder. This landscape contains some of the planet's richest soils, and the best climate to take advantage of them. Think of it: the most fertile soil in the world! And, soil scientists told me, I had some of it in my bottomlands along the creek. Even our upland soils are richer and deeper than most soils and will respond with unbelievable fertility if restored and cared for lovingly and patiently.

This land is capable of holding more species of plants and animals than any temperate wilderness. I have a hunch our cornfields could even be transformed into a paradise of flora and fauna nearly as varied as that of the tropical rainforests. That capability lies hidden from social view only by the tall corn's economic stranglehold on the farmer's mind. The fact that corn, soybeans, and wheat do so well here without irrigation is evidence that most other temperate crops would also thrive: oats (which once did), barley, rye, scores of grasses and clovers, sorghums, grain sorghum, sweet corn, popcorn, all manner of temperate fruit and nut trees, a wide variety of flowers, berries, and vegetables. (That we import asparagus and potatoes into the Corn Belt is ridiculous, and my onions are the equal of anything shipped out of Vidalia.)

There were once even hop farms here, ginseng beds, hemp fields for cordage, and tobacco crops. Native plants, wildflowers (some considered rare only because so few of us look for them between the cornfields), and beneficial herbs of myriad varieties grow here, in addition to the many weed species, some potentially useful, that humans have introduced.

Patient native plants await their time to return: where I dug a barn foundation, a strange fern that looks Jurassic grew from the dirt excavated four feet below the present woodland floor. No other ferns have grown naturally on our farm for a hundred years. I dug a tile line through the gardens, and a clump of a prairie grass common a century ago grew in the dirt left at the surface. In a nearby field where a backhoe gouged out a drainage ditch, a lovely cardinal flower grew and bloomed, a rare sight here since nearly all the wetlands have been drained—and with them the lush, game-filled cranberry bogs that greeted the pioneers. I think a cotton variety could be developed for our climate, but why do it when we can produce wool and mohair with marvelous efficiency? Not to mention milkweeds that grow wild and wildly in our fields—as children during World War II, we gathered and sold profitably the milkweed pods of silken fibers to be used to make life jackets. Today a company in Iowa is using them with feather down to improve the insulative quality of down jackets and bedspreads. We have not scratched the surface of what nature here can provide for us.

From this cornucopia of plant life spring wild animals that coexist with a full complement of cows, horses, sheep, hogs, and chickens. I have counted 130 species of wild birds living on or regularly passing through our thirty-two acres, and forty species of other wild animals. I wonder if anyone knows all the insect species here, including such rarer beauties as the luna and emperor moths and the zebra swallowtail butterfly. (I am sure that no one has identified all the species of microorganisms in the soil.)

As I work to improve the quality of the creek water, to improve the soil, to add more plant species to the farm, as the trees become more mixed in age to provide more kinds of habitat, as I renew meadow and wetland, and as the new pond in the pasture fills with fish and other aquatic life, more species will come or could be introduced. The diversity here could increase exponentially to a degree we can't yet even imagine.

If millions of humans join those of us already at this task, we can change the countryside and even most parts of the city into a patchwork quilt of Edenic garden farms supporting a stable, sustainable society in local environments so full of natural and domestic wonder, peace, and plenty that retreats to distant vacationlands would become unnecessary. This task is my life's work.

I find on my garden farm all the beauty, wonder, challenge, and satisfaction that any human could realistically ask for. I am fulfilled. I have no desire to go anywhere else or do anything else because in traveling my farm I travel the whole world, and in doing my work, I do the whole world's work.

Alison Baker

On the Roads

THE MOUNTAINS rising from the narrow valley where I live are riddled with logging roads. The hillsides are steep and the roads are switchbacks, so that as you follow one up, the same view appears again and again, expanding as you gain elevation. Finally, when you come out on a high ridge, you see the forest flowing down into the valley below, opening out here and there around a house or a pasture. In the hazy distance rises range after range of mountains, and sometimes, depending on the amount and altitude of cloud cover, you see the sudden cone of Mount McLaughlin, pale or bright or just a dim silhouette in the east.

The mountains are the Siskiyous of southern Oregon, and since we moved here two years ago I have walked the logging roads every morning with my husband and our dog. Much of this forest belongs to the Bureau of Land Management (BLM), though it's interspersed with patches of private holdings. Nearly all of it has been logged or burned, or both, at least once in the last hundred years. Most of what we walk in is a healthy second-growth forest of Douglas fir, ponderosa pine, cedar, oak, and madrone, with here and there a sugar pine. But on some cut-over upper ridges and exposed southwestern slopes not even this region's cool, wet winters can give tree seedlings enough of a start to survive the hot, dry summers, and the hills are as barren and brown as any in Utah. At the other extreme, we come now and then upon a grove of virgin firs covered with moss and lichen, trees three or four feet in diameter, as big and as old as you could hope to find at this elevation, in this climate.

The part of the forest I frequent is heavily used. In fact, the number of people who use it amazes me: loggers and hunters and government silviculturists; campers and birders and mushroom pickers; people on horseback and on four-wheelers and on mountain bikes. We actually meet people only rarely on our morning walks, but their debris is omnipresent: beer cans, strips of fluorescent plastic hanging in the trees to mark mysterious boundaries, campfire rings, and used diapers and worn-out clothes and broken stoves dumped into gullies to avoid the fifty-mile round trip to the nearest landfill, where they charge you to dump your trash. Shotgun shells and bullet casings are everywhere. Though we sometimes see hunters, more often we see the hunted—deer and jackrabbits, grouse and elk, and once a bobcat. We have yet to see a bear, but we've seen their footprints in the snow, and we've seen their late-summer scat, soft and juicy with blackberry seeds, in the middle of the road.

Like most who have come to southern Oregon from somewhere else, I like the forest because it gives me a sense of privacy and freedom. But that is an illusion. When I moved here from the city I expected to be more isolated, to have fewer dealings with people. Instead I find I have to deal with them more—or maybe just more directly. The people living in the Siskiyous are as jumbled as the mountains themselves, all of us full of our own politics and religions and ethics and plans and desires and hatreds. And there have come to be so many of us, and we all want so much that we constantly have to negotiate with each other over space, over water, over how we want to treat the animals and the creeks and the trees.

My feelings about the logging road are as complex as the populace, the geology, and the flora. I know that the roads themselves, as much as the logging they support, destroy the forest. Starting high in the mountains above my home and disrupting the whole watershed, even to the coast one hundred miles away, the roads cut through fragile, thin-soiled terrain, causing massive erosion. The culverts that run beneath them are easily blocked with branches, leaves, and dislodged rocks, so that winter rains and spring runoff overflow the ditches and wash the soil downstream, silting up streambeds and destroying salmon and trout spawning grounds. The roads require constant maintenance; every spring the BLM rescrapes, rebuilds, repacks.

But I'm not much of a bushwhacker, and I like the way the roads take me into the woods, close to birds and animals and wildflowers. I like these roads the way I like shopping malls and commercial television—I use them and I take pleasure in them, wishing all the time they didn't exist.

From ancient times the forest has served human societies as a metaphor, a representation of darkness or wildness or evil or the unknown. There are still areas of the Siskiyous, not so very far from here, where roads don't go—not many places, and not huge ones, but they're there. Incredibly rough terrain combined with hard-won pieces of legislation have made them inaccessible to people who stay on roads. These roadless areas and designated wildernesses are attempts at preserving not just watersheds and spotted owls but that ancient metaphor as well.

The forest close to my home is still a metaphor, but one that's been slashed and scraped and carved into easily accessible packages. It no longer stands for what we can't know, but for what we can do to what we don't understand. This forest is full of our roads and full of us; it is not quite a park, but it is under our control.

Once in a while my husband and I find ourselves on some road that the BLM has ceased to maintain. Depending on the location, the exposure, the soil type, it is ever so slowly being reclaimed by creeping blackberry vines, ground cones and puffballs that erupt through the gravel, bracken and fern, asters and chicory and poison oak, and by the detritus of the eroding slopes above and below it.

On such a road, when I look out into the distance and listen to an autumn wind coming down a canyon from the north and hear the golden-crowned kinglets whistling in the tops of cedars, I can feel just a touch of what the remnants of wilderness in those roadless areas still contain: a sense that, in the long run, we are surprisingly irrelevant. The marks we make, the scars we leave, the roads we cut through the mountain forests are as ephemeral, in that long run, as bear scat.

So the roads that enable us to do what we will with the forest have become metaphor themselves: they are maps through geologic time, where human beings are exactly as important as anything else on earth—no more, no less. This is a version, I think, of an old truth; a way to understand that nothing here belongs to us, and that we belong here on the same terms as the jay, a flake of gold, the ponderosa pine.

Gerald Haslam

Back in the Valley

NEAR THE SOUTHERN end of California's Great Central Valley, we veer east from Interstate 5, then travel a two-lane past the green spokes of agricultural fields, oil pumps salaaming in their midst. Soon we pass a shaggy, uncultivated plot, a ragamuffin among Lord Fauntleroys. But it is no remnant of indigenous landscape; like the farms, it is covered with nonnative plants. Everything here, it seems—weeds and crops and people—comes from somewhere else.

Wind that smells vaguely of chemicals tugs at our car. A lone kite pumps its wings above another unplanted tract. Beyond, a dust devil swerves and pirouettes, faint as a ghost, and our car rushes toward a mirage flooding the pavement: like most of California, we pursue the illusion of water.

Few of the fields here boast houses, for this is the terrain of corporate agriculture, with the richest farmers working in far-off boardrooms while brown men and women irrigate, plow, and harvest. Some family farmers remain, of course, and they live on the land and work with the laborers, who in turn reside in farm labor camps or ranch cabins or on the margin, *debajo del puente* . . . reminders of our shared past.

Well ahead of us, treeless hills begin to emerge from haze, hills steaming constantly as though Hell has sprung a leak; hot vapors are pumped underground here to melt the thick petroleum. At the foot of those hills hides a town. A few dark hints of trees betray its location but we know it well: Oildale, a community now contiguous with North Bakersfield. We discern a distant building, then two, then the silvery tangle of a refinery.

I turn to my wife and smile. "Almost home," I say.

She smiles back: "Almost home."

I have lived in many Californias—on beaches, in cities, on mountains—but only this one has gripped me as roots wrap rocks. It is far from the Golden State of imagination: no palm trees or ocean or movie stars. Here the lure is work, not leisure, and one learns quickly that life is complicated and hard. Here, too, one is constantly reminded that, no matter what humans have managed—and we have managed quite a lot—nature rules. Tule fog dense as oatmeal closes schools, dust storms close roads, heat forces folks to sprint from air conditioner to air conditioner. Yet I love this place, even with its warts showing, because I am connected.

My great-great grandparents—he a *vaquero,* she a seam-stress—first entered the Valley in the 1850s when they mi-grated north from Mexico. I was born here in 1937, married here in 1961, and will one day be buried here with my dearest friends, like our neighbors—from Oklahoma, Texas, Mis-souri, and Arkansas, mostly—who became extended family. "Speck, that clumsy kid of yours could fall out of a hole," Mr. Bundy told my dad. Then he punched my shoulder.

Yet the setting, not the people, finally dominates. Oildale is part of one of the most productive unnatural landscapes in the world. Transported water, chemical agriculture, steam-infused petroleum produce jobs for many, wealth for few. De-spite the absence of buildings, most nearby fields and hills are as developed as downtown Bakersfield.

As a kid, I used to think everywhere else smelled funny—no sulfuric belch of crude oil, no texture to the air. From my earliest memory, everything hereabouts seemed dry but not desolate. Less than six inches of rain falls most years, yet the area still teems with ants, lizards, rabbits, hawks, the whole chain. Long ago there were pronghorn and elk and grizzlies, too. And many Yokuts, native people.

When Thomas Baker migrated here in 1863, long before he made his field available to travelers, it was called Kern Island. The island—islands, really—was formed by the channels of the Kern River, whose water did not flow out of the Great Central Valley to San Francisco Bay but instead puddled nearby in two lakes, 8,300-acre Kern and 4,000-acre Buena

Vista, plus various connecting wetlands, marshes amidst desert. Only Buena Vista survived into my childhood; then it too was gone.

During those years, I often rode my bike a mile from our horned-toad neighborhood to an unreal realm I called Tarzan's House: great shading trees, dangling vines, dense brush through which animals scurried. And icy water. The Kern River and its forest were our jungle, our fishing hole, our swimming pool, and as startling in that barren setting as an unexpected flashbulb.

One day in 1950, I stood on a levee and watched brown water surge bridge-high out of the Sierra Nevada. My future wife, whose family lived near the levee in a section called Riverview, viewed the river in her living room, as her house filled with water. Neither of us could know we were witnessing the last of the floods that over millennia had deposited the alluvial soil upon which an agricultural empire was built.

Four years later, Isabella Dam was completed upstream— ostensibly for flood control, actually to provide more water for agribusiness—and the riparian forest began to die. By the time I returned home from the army in 1960, the forest's remains stood like unwrapped mummies, and the channel had become a long sand trap. My children and I walked there a few times, but they couldn't imagine the setting I described, so I tucked it back into memory.

Local folks are lobbying for the return of the year-round flows. There is reason to hope that other generations might one day know something of the natural world that once hosted the Yokuts . . . and my pals and me. In my heart—in that interior world where most of us really live—I still visit Tarzan's House, and the vacant lot where lizards scurried, and the treeless bluffs where adolescent necking thrived.

I return to Oildale frequently, and on each visit my wife and I walk its streets and alleys and fields. We try not to romanticize the past. "That park, it was an oil sump, remember? I once saw a lizard run onto it, then sink. I wanted to cry."

On our visits, we especially love to sit on the porch of my parents' old house, watch doves drinking in the gutter, and view orange-and-blue sunsets as spectacular as the northern lights. We know that air pollution creates those wondrous colors, but in Oildale everything is bittersweet.

Mary Sojourner

Spirit Level

MORE THAN ANYTHING, my father wanted me to return to our northeastern home and to the religion in which I was raised. But the high-desert mountains, dark pine and amethyst light, white water and cedar smoke where I now live is temple enough. It is one of a thousand places, some yet unknown, where if I stop to look and listen and touch, I have, for a precious time, no doubts.

What I wanted from my father was that he would know this. He would visit. We would row an old wooden boat on a twilight-still lake and fish until darkness melted around us and when we cast, we cast into mountain stars. The two of us would regain the serenity I had felt when I was a child and he rowed us out onto the evening mirror of a small Adirondack lake. As we floated on this western water I would tell him that he had taught me to find peace in wildness . . . and what had nagged between us would finally be still.

"Rocks," is what my father really said. "There's nothing out there but goddamn rocks. Why do you have to travel so far just to see a few rocks?"

In the spring of 1992, after six months of harsh and persistent wasting, my father went much further. My brother called at 1 A.M. "He died peacefully," he said. "One of the last things he asked the doctor was if it seemed to be time to get a handicapped sticker for the car." I laughed.

"Are you coming home for the service?" my brother asked.

"No," I said. "We talked about it. He said there was no point in coming all that way once he was gone."

"I don't understand," my brother said, "but it's okay."

I lit a Virgen de Guadalupe candle and set it on the porch. My dad had loved that Great Mother. Orion moved across the black sky, a breeze carried the scent of ponderosa pine. Somewhere a great horned owl gave one cry, no answer. It seemed strange to me, and comfortable, sitting on my porch, wrapped in my sleeping bag, my father's death brand-new, all held in the cool quiet off the mountains, as though my heart were cupped in a giant, stony hand. And of course, it wasn't enough.

A year later, I drove back east alone; what I needed to do could not be done in the company of anyone. I drove without music on an Oklahoma two-lane highway bordered with flame-orange gallardia and lush olive sage, below thunderheads that never broke. I camped on the banks of a dammed river and watched the mist rise into evening. Boats and RVs and people became the ghosts of a Japanese scroll. Fireflies moved in and out of the fog. I dipped my hand in the cold water, breathed in the mists and tasted river.

Next morning, deep in a limestone cave, I closed my eyes and listened to a wild little rivulet pour over stone. I set my palm flat against water caught in travertine pools and promised the owners of the cave that I would send them postcards of the blue-green falls at Havasupai.

I drove on, rolling just above the southern Missouri border. I found a little town I remembered and followed a dirt road into green light. There, in air that smells like life itself, I hiked north along the eastern bank of a river and then moved out into breast-high water. I lay back and was carried, looking up now and then to mark my way. Pebbles clicked along the bottom. I thought of the Colorado River, of how it had closed over me two years earlier and I had been so afraid. "Thank you," I whispered to the bright southern sky.

On the road a few mornings later, I looked in my rearview mirror and saw smoke from a burning field rise across a blood-red sun. White birds and black ones that might have been cormorants flew away from the fire. A dull blue iron bridge rose in front of me, pewter water stretched out below, and the

Mississippi held me for an instant exactly between my western home and my eastern birthplace. I held my breath and crossed.

I stayed alone in my parents' house. My mother was in a nursing home, but she was still present in her cooking utensils, her embroidery, her books. I cleaned the fridge and did the dishes, and when they were gleaming in the rack I walked out to her roses. I knew what was there. "He's in the roses," she had told me.

It was evening. I was washed in the warm summer twilight of childhood, in a town on a Great Lake's shoreline, on the banks of a broad river, on hilly land covered with houses and roads and shopping malls, shining with creeks and puddles and ponds. I looked down. There, at the base of those impossibly green bushes, were the shadows of my father's bones. I waited till the light was completely gone, then walked down into the basement.

It was cool there, and dark. I thought of caves, of minerals carried down and washed away. My father's tools were hung neatly on their pegs. I had never touched them. I took two screwdrivers with worn wooden handles. I reached up and grasped his spirit level, stained and dusty and, when I set it on his homemade workbench, still true. I looked at the tiny bubble catching light in fluid green as a winter southwest river. Later, I would go to the garage and find his axe and take it home to the mountains, to juniper, aspen, and pine. Axe and spirit level, work and prayer. And all those goddamn rocks.

Now, a month later, the spirit level sits above my southern window. To the north, the San Francisco Peaks hold wildflowers and prayer feathers and traces of last spring's snow. In the West, about this time of day, they are blowing up old ammunition at the abandoned army base. East, beyond my front door, the road moves out, past little rivers that run above the earth and below, curving by burned fields that sprout next fall's harvest, across that great gray water that has taken back acres of her own. I take down the level, tilt it east and west. I think of rock and water and green light, and am grateful that what brings me back to balance is just that.

Robert Crum

American Xanadu

WALKING ONE DAY along a dike in a nearby marsh (or "prairie" in the Floridian parlance), I found a smallish, elongated insect with its woody, knobbed carapace and long legs arranged like twigs on a small branch—a walking stick. As it perched on my finger, it suddenly released a little puff of mist. The mist serves as a protective mechanism: if the bug's imitation of a stick fails to fool a bird, the spray is its last defense. To a bird, it's pretty vile-smelling stuff. But for me the olfactory sensation was quite different, and I stood there in the broad light, thinking of Drambuie.

The wonders of Florida reside in such nuances, in the sway of Spanish moss in the silky morning breeze, in the white curve of a snowy egret's neck. Every available inch of this country fills in with the details of leaf and shadow by day, and the din of frog song by night. On hot, humid, summer afternoons chlorophyll seems to leak into the very air.

For a long time after I moved to the north-central part of the state, I missed what couldn't be found here: topographical variation, panoramic distances, the startling transfigurations of autumnal foliage. A geology buff, I was especially distressed by the lack of rocks. Most of Florida is a giant sandbar. The lowest areas are swamp; the highest (often only a few feet higher) are scrub. The only waterfalls begin at ground level and descend into sinks—craters where the buried limestone bedrock has dissolved and fallen away.

I am not the first to feel myself a stranger in the American subtropics. The names that the area's first white settlers gave to the landforms they came across seem, at best, to suggest their own confusion. Marshes were called prairies, and stands of trees were called hammocks. At worst, the names express a deep contempt and fear of the land. For me, the most unfortunate example of this is the name given to one of the local rivers: the River Styx—the waterway which, according to Greek mythology, the souls of the dead cross into Hades.

I now wonder if the early settlers weren't just annoyed that this land wasn't as compliant as others they had known. But those who came with different intentions found a different country. One of the early explorers of the region was William Bartram. I often think of him as a kind of Mozart of a naturalist, not because of his prose style, which tended to be prolix and grandiose, but because of his talent for turning common themes (clouds, streams, flowers) into evidence of Heaven on Earth. An ecstatic from the word go, he relates how the hooves of his horse turned red after riding through mile after mile of wild strawberries. He swooned over flowers and gloried in the mammocumulus cloudscapes that are this region's substitute for mountains. He especially loved the big, turquoise-sided springs that percolate up through the limestone.

Samuel Coleridge happened to be reading Bartram's *Travels in Florida* just before writing his visionary poem "Kubla Khan." It is often noted that the creative spark for that work was opium, Coleridge's drug of choice, but it's not generally known that much of the imagery derives from Bartram's descriptions of Florida. Today Coleridge's "caverns measureless to man" are popular spots for scuba divers. Some of the cool streams that issue from the springs, which flow "five miles meandering with a mazy motion through wood and dale," are crowded with inner-tubers in summer. But during the rest of the year, those "deep romantic chasms" usually belong to those few who take the time to visit.

One recent afternoon I took my canoe out on the River Styx. It was a bright day toward the end of spring, and I paddled as far as I could, until the river spread into a swamp. From there it was a matter of poling the canoe and getting out to lift it over logs. From all that I saw, this was not a river in Hell. Squadrons of white ibis worked the shoreline, drilling their curved red bills into the muck. Overhead, a rare wood stork spread its black and white wings. The alligators seemed surprised to have had their pleasure dome found out, and splashed into the water like huffy senators. The columns of bald cypress towered skyward, and their reflections in the water, mixed with blue sky and green foliage, gave the illusion of as much light and space below as there was above.

I have seen rivers that could qualify as Stygian, but those—high in fecal content and toxic waste—are not works of nature. Fortunately, there are no such rivers around here. If Heaven has a local address, I think it may well be a spot such as this, where the insects smell of expensive liqueurs and the mockingbird, after a particularly long, beautiful riff (according to Bartram), "springs into the air as though to retrieve its soul." The limestone below the sand is two miles thick. Sharks' teeth wash out of the soil after every deluge. And after every bout of withering summer humidity, the afternoon thunderstorms bring raindrops big enough to knock you over.

Tim McNulty

Island of Rivers

T HE SNOWMELT STREAM rippled brightly beneath
the mossy trunks of fallen trees, paused in a rock-walled
pool, then riffled over a gallery of polished boulders into
sunlight. The quick splashes of silver in a side channel across
the river were hard to see in all that light. But following my
pointing arm, my five-year-old daughter gave a shout when
she saw them. "Salmon!"

We spent the rest of the afternoon wading in bouldery
shadows near the shore as the first Graywolf River pinks made
the summer climb to their spawning gravels in the deep, un-
broken forests of Washington's Olympic Mountains. The
Graywolf pinks are unique among the wild swimmers, returning earlier and climbing higher than other pink-salmon

runs in the Northwest. Because they spawn only in odd-numbered years, I was anxious for my daughter to see them. Caitlin was too young to pay them much attention on their last visit, and another cycle seemed too long to wait. We camped that night beneath valley-bottom trees and listened as the stream whispered its news.

More than a dozen rivers rise in the glaciers and snowfields that mantle the mountainous heart of the Olympic Peninsula, radiating outward like the silvery spokes of a wheel. Each river has its own character, its own mix of forest and wildlife communities, and its distinctive races of wild salmon.

Salmon are the bearers of gifts to these islandlike mountains and forests. In the downhill flow of rain and snow from the Pacific, they alone return valuable nutrients leached from the soil and flushed out to the sea. Returning salmon meant survival for the original inhabitants of these coastal valleys. Upon ascending the rivers of their birth, salmon spawn, laying and fertilizing their eggs in clean-washed river gravels before they die. Not only does this heroic expenditure ensure the continuance of their kind, but their spent carcasses remain to feed a host of terrestrial wildlife. Bald eagles, black bears, river otters, mink, even the diminutive winter wren and deer mouse share in this seasonal banquet that will help see them through the critical months of winter.

Of the many rivers that drain this range, the Graywolf holds a special magic for me. One of the last unroaded low-elevation valleys, its steep, rugged slopes were a refuge for gray wolves before they were hunted and trapped to extinction in the 1920s. The valley was still unscarred by logging a half-century later when I first came to the peninsula to live.

Before long, I had plunged into a prolonged effort to help save the Graywolf Valley—and several others here—from the designs of a cadre of road engineers and timber-sales specialists in the employ of the United States Forest Service. A decade of letters, articles, meetings, public hearings, and the support of countless individuals saw the lower Graywolf Valley protected as part of the national wilderness system. (The upper watershed, along with close to a million acres of the mountainous interior of the Olympic Peninsula, was already protected as part of Olympic National Park.)

That fall my partner, Mary, and I hiked to a favorite spot in the canyon where the river spills its light around a garden of mossy boulders. There, in the company of some close friends, we were married. This past fall those same friends joined us on the river for our tenth anniversary. We read poems and raised cups of hot sake as moonlight crept down the canyon wall.

Tonight the moon is a thin crescent. From our porch in the foothills, I look out over a low, timbered ridge to a gap that drops into Graywolf Canyon. Beyond it, the snowy summits of Graywolf Ridge ripple off into the interior mountains. Caitlin still gets the names of the peaks mixed up, and she sometimes confuses one river we hiked with another. It's understandable; there are so many ribboning their way down the coast, and their names, taken from the native people who still

live at their mouths, are hard for her to remember: Skoko-
mish, Queets, Quillayute, Quinault.

But memories enfold the heart like rings of a tree, and our
roots here deepen with each winter's rain. Each year Caitlin is
able to backpack a little farther into these mountains, and this
summer we reached a milestone. From High Divide we
looked across the upper Hoh River to Mount Olympus, the
highest central peak. Its glaciers gleamed ice-blue in the afternoon light, and the soft rumble of their gathered meltwaters
reached us from a mile below.

Earlier this fall I accompanied Caitlin's first-grade class to
the Dungeness River, into which the Graywolf flows. We
talked about the chinook salmon, *Tyee* or "Chief" to the coast
people. Development pressures, irrigation withdrawals, and
erosion from logging in the foothills have taken a toll on the
lower river, and the chinook are not faring well. Fewer than
twenty returned this year to spawn. As we searched among
river stones for caddis-fly and stone-fly larvae, Caitlin spotted
some wintering coho salmon fry in the shallows. Like the children, these small salmon spend their formative time in their
home watersheds before swimming out to explore their North
Pacific world. In two years, the indelible imprint of these waters will lead them precisely back.

It's this kind of connection I try to nurture in my daughter.
Not to lead her back to this place necessarily—though I'd be
thrilled if she chose to live here—but to help her find her
home ground wherever she lives. I want her to know these is-

lands of childhood as part of a larger island, and the rivers that drain them as the arms of a single sea. Like salmon, our children's gift will be to bring their gathered riches back to a land made poor by taking and plant them among the winter wrens and newly greening trees.

Christopher Merrill

What I Do
Not Own

INDIAN SUMMER. Coyotes start howling a little after daybreak, and all along the canyon—*El Cajón Grande,* four miles north of Santa Fe—dogs, goats, and burros respond in kind. By midmorning my neighbor's macaw is squawking in its cage. Magpies glide through the apple orchard out front. The sky? Cerulean, as it is more than three hundred days a year in New Mexico. Beyond the gate behind our house is Santa Fe National Forest; up on the mesa, a five-minute walk away, cinnamon bears are once again foraging too close to civilization. Three years ago more than thirty bears were caught in these hills and transported north to the woods near Chama. One morning my neighbor woke up my wife and me to show us the large sow that Fish and Game officers had trapped in his backyard. The odds of a female surviving transplantation that late in the season were small, and he tried in vain to break the lock on the barrel-shaped cage.

"Another day in paradise!" cries Hans-Mukh, the Sikh day laborer who takes care of a neighboring orchard. A transplant himself (from Pittsburgh), he is walking up the driveway, hauling horse manure to spread around the aging trees, his white turban bunched up over his ears so that he can fit a Walkman headset around the back of his head. The orchard belongs to Percival King, a spry man in his eighties who helped build the atomic bomb in nearby Los Alamos. He is the *mayordomo,* or manager, of our *acequia,* our irrigation ditch, and I like to joke that ours is the best-regulated ditch in the state. Every spring Hans-Mukh and I spend an afternoon walking the acequia, clearing leaves and brush and broken branches, then ushering in the water diverted for the growing season from Tesuque Creek. Unlike other neighbors who sometimes join us for part of the journey downstream, Hans-Mukh and I do not belong to the landed gentry, and so we do not treat our labor as a pleasant distraction. It is part of our job.

As the caretaker of the estate surrounding me, I live in a small adobe cottage that once housed chickens. As a writer struggling to make ends meet, I am grateful for the gift of free rent. What is more, I enjoy the work integral to maintaining this place—pruning shrubs and trees; gardening in a variety of flower, wildflower, vegetable, and perennial beds; planting bulbs in the fall, raking leaves, and splitting wood for the winter; cleaning chimneys; walking the ditch. This work is, indeed, a vital counter to my literary activities, my inner life, what the poet William Matthews calls "this quarantine, / reading and pacing and feeding the fireplace."

But there are other reasons for living among orchards and horses, piñons and junipers, saltbrush and sage. "I learn from everything I do not own," John Hay writes, and I am heartened by his counsel. My wife and I own nothing here—not these three acres that real-estate agents covet, nor the water rights in continuous litigation, nor the house we guard, nor the artwork adorning the walls, nor the swimming pool we watch over as if it were a sick child. We work for our housing: a simple trade.

The question of ownership extends to the natural world. Certainly the Tesuque Indians living a few miles to the west have a different understanding of man's proper relation to nature than might exist among our neighbors. No one "owns" these cottonwoods turning gold and groaning in the earth, arcing over the acequia and our house. Nor the lawn I cut every five days until the first snow, grass native to worlds far from the foothills of the Sangre de Cristo Mountains. Nor the garter snake sunning on the flagstone path leading to the main house, a thick coil preparing to hibernate. Nothing is ours.

This is what my immersion here has taught me: like the

flash floods, which routinely carve the arroyo behind us and which once dumped more than a ton of mud in the swimming pool, everything flows away, even in the high desert. Our tenure anywhere is brief; as we attend to our surroundings, we must not fool ourselves into believing that we own anything beyond our capacity for love and awe.

What I treasure here in autumn are the magpies feeding in the orchard, the red-shafted flicker drumming on the *viga* above our door, the scat of the mountain lion I have yet to see, the bears that will escape this year's traps, the aspens blazing in the distance. At sunset on the mesa, when the coyotes howl again and the sky bleeds above the Jemez Mountains to the west and north, I can see the lights of Los Alamos as well as the first stars flickering overhead. A strange match. Yet this spectacle is what will send me to my study later in the evening, where I will write, praying for vision, compassion, and genuine acts of imagination, which belong to no one—and to us all.

Ken Wright

Married, with Mountains

TOMORROW, TOM LEAVES for Mexico. So tonight we share a twelve-pack under a cold January sky. With the temperature in the low twenties, we sit like a couple of lookouts on the bridge of an icebreaker, wrapped in thick jackets, gloves, and hats. From a beat-up sofa on a friend's porch we keep watch over a dark side street in Durango, Colorado.

In the morning, Tom will get a ride down through New Mexico to Nogales. There he will hop a train to Mexico City and begin a four-month hitchhiking journey through Latin America.

"I can't believe you're going to have a kid," he says. He follows this with a deep swig of beer, as if he's rinsing those funky-tasting words from his mouth. "Do you know what you're doing?" He looks out across the street at a yellow-and-white Victorian house, a survivor from the days of Durango's mining boom. "I can't imagine having a kid," he says. "Or a wife." His frosty breath dissipates, but the words hang in the air.

I respond with a sip of beer and a glance out over the trenches that January's snow has made of the streets. I think about what lies ahead for Tom, but I don't worry, because my friend is a traveler. And he shouldn't worry about me, because I am—still—a traveler, too.

Sure, these days I don't cover as much ground as Tom. The only time I went to Mexico I swam, across the Rio Grande. I stood there among the agave and Mexican cow pies for a few *momentitos,* then swam back. And I don't hitchhike much since the afternoon I waited quietly in the backseat of a Delta 88, my feet resting on beer cans and a shotgun, while two drunken madmen debated whether to let me out or not. I think that was when my walking career really took off.

Every morning I walk down the dirt driveway to the pavement, which I follow around the corner into the valley where the elk like to winter. I check the flow in the ditch; I inspect the foliage on the scrub oaks; I examine the color of the sandstone bluffs. In the afternoon I may return there, saunter along the same route. On weekends I usually make it up some nearby hill like the rampart of cliffs behind our house or the unnamed ridge ribboned with logging roads on the other side the valley. Sometimes my wife, Sarah, and I venture into the high country where I pull out the fishing pole for a few hours or we walk up above treeline to wander across the tundra. But I rarely get too far from home anymore. I don't want to.

The difference between Tom and me is that Tom is a bachelor traveler, and I am a married traveler. I'm not referring to legal marital status; I mean that I have made the same oath of loyalty, fidelity, and obligation to this landscape that I made to Sarah: *I will stay with you, learn about you, accept you for who you are.*

My spouse is the Colorado Plateau, its mountains—the San Juans, the La Platas, the Abajos, and the Sleeping Ute—and its rivers—the Animas, the San Juan, the Dolores, the Piedra. I am also bound to what I encounter daily, the streets, hills, mesas, and foothills that surround my town. I am connected to the people who live, play, work, and muddle through here faithfully. Like any marriage, this terrestrial relationship is ever-evolving, sometimes moody, often routine, filled with tedious chores. I must constantly rally the energy to seek the new and relish the familiar.

But tonight, I don't say any of this to Tom, and he is quiet as he hands me another can of beer. On the street in front of us a woman walks by, shuffling her feet, her arms wrapped around herself. She coughs twice, and two little bursts of steam shine under a streetlight. I pull my cap lower over my head to keep my thoughts in and the deepening cold out. Yes, my friend, I tell Tom in my mind, I travel every day. I have changed only the direction of my travel. I walk these trails with a traveler's spirit, I hunger for awareness, adventure, knowledge, and challenge. And I have not been disappointed.

Should I say these things to Tom? Ramble on to him about my marriage-to-a-big-ol'-plateau philosophy? He might understand that, but what makes him grab his backpack is the thought of the traditional marriage-to-a-person, the bambino-on-the-way that seem to accompany squatting in one place too long. How would I explain to him that my wife and our fledgling family are an inseparable part of my marriage to this place?

Maybe I should tell a story: "My father loved to go to the woods of northern New England," I'll begin, and then I'll tell him about how up there, in the hardwoods, on the ancient, rounded mountains, around the lakes and creeks, my father taught me to fish and hunt and walk. While we walked, my father would tell me about the land around us, about how slopes with bedrock outcroppings meant good trout pools, about how an autumn-yellow beech grove meant whitetail scrounging for beechnuts.

As we approached those places, my father grew more respectful, pensive, and alert than I ever saw him anywhere else. He would slow his pace, move precisely, step deliberately. I would imitate him as he slid each leg forward, touched his toes to the ground, and rolled his foot flat so the leaves made no sound. It was then that I learned how to walk. It was then I realized that I had learned all I know about the land by how I passed through it.

This is what I want to show to my child.

In the end, I don't offer Tom any of these explanations. I just smile to myself, and accept another beer.

Brenda Peterson

Bread Upon
the Waters

"Seagulls memorize your face," the old man called
out to me as he strode past on his daily walk. I stood on
the seawall feeding the flock of gray-and-white gulls who
also make this Puget Sound beach their home. "They know
their neighbors." He tipped his rather rakish tweed motoring
cap and kept walking fast. "Can't let the heartbeat stop," he
explained.

I meet this man many days on the beach. We rarely talk; we
perform our simple chores: I feed the seagulls and say prayers,
he keeps his legs and his heart moving. But between us there is
an understanding that these tasks are as important as anything

else in our lives; maybe they even keep us alive. Certainly our relationship with each other and with this windswept northwest beach is more than a habit. It is a bond, an unspoken treaty we've made with the territory we call home.

For ten years I have migrated from beach shack to cabin, moving along the shore like the native tribes that once encircled all of Puget Sound. But unlike the first people who loved this wild, serpentine body of cold water, my encampments have changed with the whim of my landlords rather than with the seasons. Somehow mixed up in my blood of Seminole, Swede, and French-Canadian Indian is my belief that I may never own land even if one day I might be able to afford it. Ownership implies possession; as much as I revere this inland sea, she will never belong to me. Why not, then, belong to her?

Belong. As a child the word mesmerized me. Because my father's forestry work moved us every other year—from southern piney woods to soaring Montana spruce to High Sierra fir—the landscape seemed in motion. To *be long* in one place was to take deep root like other settled folk, or like the trees themselves, the Standing People, as my father called them. There was also that elegiac and open-hearted *longing* in belonging that even today, after a decade settling on the shores of Puget Sound, hasn't been sated in me. After I have lived a long life on this beach, I hope that someone might someday say, "She belonged here," as much as the purple starfish that cling to rock crevices covered in algae fur.

The Hopi Indians of Arizona believe that our daily rituals

and prayers literally keep this world spinning on its axis. For me, feeding the seagulls is one of those everyday prayers. When I walk out of my front door and cross the street to the seawall, they caw welcome, their wings almost touching me as they sail low over my shoulders, then hover overhead, midair. Sometimes if it's been raining, their feathers flick water droplets onto my face like sprinklings of holy water. The brave fliers swoop over the sea and back to catch the bread in their beaks inches above my hand. Then the cacophonic choir—gulls crying and crows *kak-kak*ing as my special sidearm pitch sends tortillas whizzing through the air, a few of them skipping across the waves like flour Frisbees. The acrobatic catch of the day is rewarded with whatever dessert I've saved.

I am not the only neighbor who has fed these gulls. For three years, two afternoons a week a green taxi pulled alongside the beach. From inside, an ancient woman, her back bent like the taut arch of a crossbow, would lean out of the car window and call in a clear, tremulous soprano. The seagulls recognized the sun-wrinkled, almost blind face she raised to them. She smiled and said to the taxi driver, "They *know* I'm here."

It was always the same driver, the same ritual—a shopping bag full of day-old bread donated by a local baker. "She told me she used to live by the sea," the driver explained to me once. "She don't remember much else about her life . . . not her children, not her husband." Carefully the driver would tear each bread slice into four squares the way the woman requested. "Now she can't hardly see these birds. But she hears them and she smells the sea. Calls this taking her medicine."

Strong medicine, the healing salt and mineral sea this old woman took into her body and soul twice a week. She lived in the nursing home at the top of our hill, and every time I saw the familiar ambulance go by I prayed it was not for Our Lady of the Gulls.

This fall, when wild hurricanes shook the South and drought seized the Northwest, the old woman stopped coming to our beach. I waited for her all autumn, but the green taxi with its delighted passenger never came again. I took to adding two weekly afternoon feedings to my own morning schedule. These beach meetings are more mournful, in memory of the old woman whose name I never knew, who didn't remember her own name, who remembered only the gulls.

Not long afterward my landlady called with the dreaded refrain: "House sold, must move on." I walked down to the beach and opened my arms to the gulls. With each bread slice I said a prayer that Puget Sound would keep me near her. One afternoon I got the sudden notion to drive down the sound. There I found a cozy white cottage for rent, a little beach house that belongs to an old man who'd lived on this promontory since the 1940s. A stroke had sent him to a nursing home, and the rent from his cottage would pay for his care.

Before I moved one stick of furniture into the house, I stood on the beach and fed the gulls in thanksgiving. They floated above my head; I felt surrounded by little angels. Then I realized that these were the very same gulls from two miles down the beach near my old home—there was that bit of fishline wrapped around a familiar webbed foot, that wounded wing, and the distinct markings of a young gray gull, one of my favorite high fliers.

Who knows whether the old man was right? The seagulls may have memorized my face and followed me—but I had also, quite without realizing it, memorized them. And I knew then that I was no newcomer here, not a nomad blown by changeable autumn winds. It is not to any house, but to this beach I have bonded. I belong alongside this rocky inlet with its salt tides, its pine-tiered, green islands, its gulls who remember us even when we've forgotten ourselves.

Gary Snyder

The Watershed

Twenty-five years ago I found myself crawling with a compass through a manzanita thicket on a forested slope in the northern Sierra Nevada. I was trying to locate at least two of the boundaries to a parcel of land that some friends wanted me to buy in on; eventually I found the brass cap that established a corner. I had never been in that part of the Sierra before, but I recognized the community: ponderosa pine, incense cedar, black oak, Douglas fir, madrone, the occasional sugar pine. Lots of manzanita. A wild meadow full of native bunchgrass. Knowing these characters and their ways from other regions, and remembering that I liked them, I said yes.

Two grown sons, two stepdaughters, three cars, two trucks,

four buildings, one pond, two well pumps, close to a hundred chickens, seventeen fruit trees, and about ninety cords of firewood later, I'm totally a part of this plain Sierra forest world. And I'm still a cheerful beginner and learner, noticing things every year that somehow hung back earlier. (There is one boundary down in the chaparral that I still haven't located.) This area hasn't changed that much in a quarter-century—though the developments are getting closer—but my sense of where I am sure has.

We are on a gentle ridge at the three-thousand-foot elevation, with the gorge of the South Yuba River to the south. The drainage of Shady Creek and some old hydraulic gold-mining diggings are to the north, and beyond that the Middle and North Yuba rivers. The ridge is part of the three-pronged Yuba River watershed, between the Feather and American rivers. Some of the watershed is in Nevada County. It goes from near sea level to more than nine thousand feet. Our place is on the part called San Juan Ridge.

The ridge is all forested, but it's not a pristine wilderness. Talks with local ranchers and lumbermen indicate that it was logged at least once in this century, and has gone through at least one major fire and countless small ones. But population is spread thin, and the wild is at work all around us. Pines grow surprisingly tall in seventy years, the deer herds are resilient, cougar have come back, black bear leave pawprints on woodshed refrigerators, and bobcats, coyotes, and foxes sometimes stroll by in broad daylight. Even the diggings, which were two thousand acres of pure gravel desert a century ago—stripped of soil by giant nozzles washing out the scattered gold—are colonized by hardy manzanita, bonsai-looking pine, and some other highly adapted plants. Wild nature is tough.

The first major environmental conflict in California was between Sacramento Valley farmers and the hydraulic gold miners of the Yuba. Judge Lorenzo Sawyer's 1884 decision banned absolutely all release of mining debris into the watershed—it was the end of hydraulic mining here. We know now that the amount of material transported out of the ierra into the valley river systems and onto good farmlands was eight times the amount of dirt removed for the Panama Canal.

The county's boosters still seem to take more pleasure in the romance of the gold era than in the subsequent processes of restoration. The Sierra foothills are still described as "Gold Country," the highway is called "49," the businesses are called "Nugget" and "Bonanza." I have nothing against gold—I wear it in my teeth and in my ear—but the real wealth here is the great Sierra forest. That is a source of controversy too, and my neighbors and I have sat in on many long-range management-plan hearings and had lengthy and complicated arguments with silviculturalists, district rangers, and all sorts of experts from the local national forest. The vast stretches of forested ridges we can see from the nearest high point are all bureaucratically accounted for. They are all surveyed and broken into mosaics of public and private ownership: Tahoe

National Forest, Sierra Pacific Land Company, Bureau of Land Management, and various private holdings. For the time, those designations grant various "rights." But with only "rights" and no land ethic, these summer-dry forests could be irreversibly degraded into chaparral over the coming centuries.

County-mandated codes, state-mandated fire regulations, suburban-styled building codes, Forest Service management plans—there is plenty of government. The thinly populated, healthy Sierra foothill forestlands are valued for watershed, for timber production, as wildlife habitat and back-to-nature haven; but above all they are treated as real estate. Development, not gold or lumber, is the business of the foothill counties. Being a committed inhabitant of a place like this is cause for perpetual vigilance as one gets caught between the developers, the county, and the logging sales. But I'd choose no place else. And there is no place else, no matter how remote, where the same dialectic of exploitation and conservation is not at play.

We dream of cultural as well as ecological restoration. I recite the words from the lost Nisenan language for deer (*k'uti*), cougar (*pekun*), and pine (*'inimim*), hoping to honor a little of the ancient history that was here before the rush for gold. My family and I venture out any week of the year to scramble off the roads and trails through canyons and ridges, always learning new plants, new birds, and occasionally finding a "corner," the survey pipes that are also part of our game. The diggings, those horrible scars from mining, we have come to see as complex, vital landscapes with canyons, hidden creeks, and bogs—largely wetlands, in fact. The public lands are the people's lands, if we make them so.

No matter how many grids of ownership are projected, no matter how many "uses" are permitted, there is always that opening which is wildness, impermanence, unpredictability, contingency, freedom. Screech owls in the spring night, flickers swooping off between oaks, coyotes, nuthatches, band-tailed pigeons—there is a year-round rising of little calls and yowls that is dampened only by storms. On a day of really clear air, the view from an open place on Bald Mountain sweeps east from the Sierra crest all around west across the Sacramento Valley to the skyline of the Coast Ranges.

None of this vivid natural performance is exceptional; it is normal, and universal. And so is the political vigilance it takes to be a member of this place. In one sense it is all just more layers of text on the rich old narrative of wild nature.

John Haines

Descent

W HY WE DO A certain thing rather than another, when it would seem that a number of
choices lie open to us, can be a matter for a lifetime
of thought, and we would still not have arrived at a final
answer.

In my student days in New York, in the early 1950s, when I
was far from any sort of mature work or outlook, still puzzling
out my life from day to day and from month to month, the
reading I had undertaken ranged through the whole of modern poetry in English, with initial forays into Spanish and
German poetry, as well as the better part of modern and classi-
cal literature generally—the novels, the short stories and
plays, along with the many critical commentaries. For reasons
easily understood, considering my earlier venture to Alaska,

that reading included also a good deal of work from Scandinavian literatures—from Sweden, Iceland, Norway, and Denmark—and I refer here to the work of such writers as Knut Hamsun, Jens Peter Jacobsen, and Sigrid Undset.

Amid all of this reading and study, there was one text above all that gained a life interest for me, and that was William Carlos Williams's *In the American Grain.* An idiosyncratic collection of essays on American history, influenced certainly by D. H. Lawrence's *Studies in Classic American Literature,* a book it closely resembles, the essays range from discovery through colonial times, focusing now and again on figures like Daniel Boone, Aaron Burr, and Samuel Houston, who were, or seemed to be, at odds with the prevailing winds of conquest and settlement.

The main theme of the book is the discovery, if only potential, of that true ground underfoot—the one inherent thing in our history, discounted then as now by all but a few. And the essay that in many respects held the most enduring interest for me was a brief thing of four pages called "Descent." Its substance can be felt in the following quotation:

"The primitive destiny of the land is obscure. . . . Through that stratum of obscurity the acute but frail genius of the place must penetrate. . . . I speak of esthetic satisfaction. This want, in America, can only be filled by knowledge, a poetic knowledge, of that ground."

And elsewhere in that essay I found this potent instruction: "It is imperative that we sink."

I took those words, and others like them, literally as well as symbolically; they seemed at the time to be meant for me alone. When I returned to Alaska in 1954, to my home region of Richardson, still isolated nearly seventy miles by road from Fairbanks, I made the decision—though I could not have articulated it as I do now—to let go, to sink into that country, accept it on its own terms, and make of it what I could. Among those steep hills of birch and aspen, on the fire-scarred spruce ridges and windswept domes, in the bogs and alder-tangled creek bottoms; in the Tanana River islands, sandbars, and channels; in the early snowfall and late spring, the long nights of midwinter and the long light of midsummer—in its scattered, transitory human history also—I found my place in which to settle, in the true sense, and everything has grown from that.

As it was the interior of that country—closed in by the Alaska Range to the south, by the Arctic Range to the north, and by the many domes and ridges of the interlying hills—so it was my own interior I set out to explore, with the aid of a few books and with the countryside itself open before me: that aesthetic ground from which all art and literature draw their nourishment, a soil in its own right and, unlike this material earth, inexhaustible.

I might have settled elsewhere and become a different man and writer. The decision was, if you will, in part accident, or it may have been that thing we call fate. I have responded at one time or another to the seashore, to its tidal pools and unique forms of aquatic life; and to the rocks and painted caves of a semi-desert mountain complex. The woodlands of the eastern United States have appealed to me in another way, both familiar and strange. Not long ago, returning to Fairbanks by road from Anchorage, we drove over a rough mountain pass where the countryside, incredibly green with mosses and late summer shrubs, and with numerous outcroppings of rock, reminded me strongly of the Yorkshire moors and the Scottish Highlands, land I had come to know insufficiently during a year's stay in northern England. There too, in a land long settled, bearing the marks of an older pastoral society, a part of me came briefly to feel at home.

But beyond all of these lay that apparently inevitable to-be-discovered region, the boreal forest; and beyond that, the open distance of that landscape left behind by the icefields, and from which, in the course of a dozen thousand years or so, much of the rest has come.

From where does it come, this felt familiarity, of land and space? I do not know for a certainty, though I have more than once attempted to define it. In a letter written years ago to a fellow writer, I expressed it in the following way:

"When we look out on that high and open tundra with its scattered ponds and grassy mounds, I think our attention to it has little to do with an ideal, but rather with a memory, so embedded in our consciousness that we respond to it without quite understanding why. If, as I believe, that landscape corresponds to an original setting for humanity, and if in some part of ourselves we have remained open to it, then our response to the land has a sensible explanation; and imagination, released by those contours and details, awakens, and the mind finds a true home for a moment."

I believe this to be close to the truth, and as close as we are likely to get.

But to descend implies that one must eventually climb, emerge from that place of descent, bearing whatever gift or insight one may have gained. After years of instructive isolation in that interior country, I returned, to reenter that other life I had left behind and had almost forgotten. And I have, not without initial difficulty, come to accept and like the city where I find it, a walkable and convenient place to be, with its own character, necessary to humanity as any stone-walled field or neighboring copse.

So much, briefly, for my own natural history. Meanwhile, and always, there is that other America—the persistent face of wealth and privilege, of ownership and political hierarchy; this self-devouring enterprise that admits no limits to its conquest of nature, to its right to exploit every known resource, and which even now refuses to restrain its appetite. This industrial maggot burrowing into the "last frontier," as if a people could not rest and thrive if that American mirage, the frontier, ceased to exist. But it is already disappearing, exists perhaps now as a kind of tinted vacationland, an immense outdoor theater. And I believe we will learn to live with its absence or perish, as a nation, as a people.

In writing this, I recall the provocative concluding sentence of Williams's essay: "However hopeless it may seem, we have no other choice: we must go back to the beginning; it must all be done over."

Consider those words as you will—in the sense of a history to be retold with a firmer affection for the truth, as I think Williams intended, and as difficult as it may seem and will always be. That is the task of the writer, the poet, the artist; of all of us who in one way or another labor to make of this damaged but still resilient earth a saner and better place.

And once again, and with my own experience in mind, beyond most of our fleeting temporal concerns, lies that other, parallel country of imagination, that knows no geographical or political boundaries, and where a writer, a poet, is free to roam, to settle and build as he can.

Kathleen Norris

The Lands of Sunrise and Sunset

I MUST LIVE HERE because of the quiet. On my dawn walk last Saturday the world was so still that I began to wonder if the nearly full moon, still high in the western sky, was about to speak. Eventually I heard several vehicles in the distance—no more than three in the forty-five minutes I was out—and I caught a little movement to the south of the highway that turned out to be five whitetail deer. Stopped, watching me, wary. One stood behind a round hay bale so that just its ears showed—the Charlie Chaplin of deerdom. Back in town, the only moving thing was a girl delivering newspapers.

This morning it was snowing, and the world was even more still, more drawn into itself as the sky fell. Tomorrow sun is forecast—our winter skies can be surprisingly bright, as blindingly blue as in high autumn. Maybe I endure the winters here because of the blue light. A seasoned television cameraman—he'd worked on assignment for CBS all over the world—once told me that our snowy plains and sky had the bluest light he'd ever seen. When I was six months old I spent long hours in a hospital crib and probably had what people now describe as the "near-death experience" of wandering down a tunnel of light. Ever since, I've been drawn toward blue. The frustration of having had this intensity of experience long before I had words for it is probably what made me a writer.

And I live here because no one in Lemmon, South Dakota, thinks that being a writer is a big deal. They regard me with a healthy mix of pride and wariness. But if my neighbor the cop is up early, ready to start the day shift, and he happens to notice that the light is on in my studio, I'm just another person doing my chores. If a rancher delivering calves to the local livestock auction sees me walking by at 6 A.M., he knows that in some obscure way, I'm working too, up at that hour because that's when the job gets done.

I live here because, after being out in what is purported to be "the real world," after too much business travel and literary hoohah, this is a good place to come home to. At its very best it becomes my monastery, which progresses like a river by running in place, its currents strong and life-sustaining. This is my real world, where life proceeds at its own healthy pace, where I can revel in the luxury of paying more attention to sunrise and sunset than to clock time.

Yet I'm still a city person by South Dakota standards, because I live in a town of 1,600 that is by far the largest "city" in the enormous northwestern quarter of South Dakota. Country people are those who live on ranches forty miles from town, along gravel section-line roads. In winter they stock up, because it may be a week or more before they can get to a grocery or hardware store. But in more than twenty years of living here I've become enough of a prairie person to feel hemmed in by the houses and tree-lined streets surrounding me. Most of the trees in town were planted when my mother was a child, but I've become a throwback to an earlier generation. At least once a day I need to walk the three blocks to the edge of town and see the land, see how the sky is playing with the horizon.

I often think I live here because I'm a frustrated painter, drawn to painting this landscape with words. And even when I'm not writing about this place, when I'm writing a memoir of my twenties in New York City, or trying to recall the religious sense of the world I had as a child, it is the sunrises and sunsets here that ground me in the present.

Not long ago, I spent three days immersed in grueling work, writing a personal narrative that seemed too personal, too painful to ever see the light of day. Sitting with my notes around me, gazing at a blank computer screen, I felt as if I were being jabbed repeatedly by a dull knife. A deadline loomed, and I was still spending hours just sitting and brooding, letting the thing work itself out in me.

When I finally finished shaping the first draft and knew that I was well on my way toward completing it, it was just past five in the afternoon. Glancing outside for the first time in hours, I noticed that the sky was doing glorious, brilliant things. I pulled on my boots and a jacket, and began walking west, toward one of those sunsets in which both the eastern and western sky is vivid with color—dawn in reverse, gold gone to peach gone to scarlet. And as I walked I began to have a biblical sense of God's presence in the sky, of God speaking through the colors. It seemed a blessing not only on the day and the coming night, but on the closure of this particular piece of writing, which I'd been trying to draw out of my heart and onto paper for seven years.

As I've spent so much time immersed in Benedictine liturgy, of which the psalms are the mainstay, I know many of their phrases by heart. One of the goals of monastic life is to let the psalms become so much a part of one's consciousness that they surface unexpectedly, in response to a blessing or a curse; to the presence of either evil or good in the circumstances of daily life. As I walked on that afternoon I suddenly recalled a blessing from Psalm 21: "The Lord will bless your going and your coming, your resting and rising forevermore."

It is the aim of contemplative living, at least in the Christian mode, to learn to recognize a blessing when you see one and to respond to it with words that God has given you. *Yes,* in response to that wildly colorful yet peaceful sky; *yes,* I could say back to God a line from Psalm 65: "The lands of sunrise and sunset you fill with joy."

Andrei Codrescu

City Nature

M Y NATURE IS the city. Not any city: only those cities, like New Orleans, that have become nature. Here, there are doors older than most American trees, street corners dense with the psychic substance of past events, manhole covers that can be read like a natural formation. This kind of city accrues a nature to itself over time: doors are trees, street corners are hot springs, manhole covers are arroyos. Forms become organic through use: who can deny that jazz can have the force of wind, or that café au lait at Kaldi's on a rainy day is possessed of duration?

I am arguing, I suppose, against the hackneyed opposition between "nature" and "civilization," with its residues of guilt and recrimination. Sure, at some point doors replaced trees, but that was a (relatively) long time ago. Long enough, anyway, for weeds to crack through the cobblestones, and for flowers, vines, grass, live oaks, palms, figs, and banana trees to grow and disappear. Long enough for the resident life forms to reach a *modus vivendi,* to change and die and be remembered and forgotten. The peculiar thing about human "nature" is its ability to regret its past, when nature was more "natural." And cities are the centers, par excellence, of this regret. I doubt very much if human beings bereft of this city-born nostalgia could even have a feeling for nature. I'm not talking about ideology (that human thing) here but about sentiment (that natural thang). The point is that both "nature" and "civilization" are metaphors. It cannot be otherwise: we can only understand where we live through how we feel about it. If we love it and it makes us feel good, it's "nature." Otherwise, it's the "state," or "civilization."

New Orleans is a creature of the river, much as Egypt (before the Aswan Dam) used to be a creature of the Nile. At night, when you can't sleep because the above paradox keeps you awake, you hear the whistles and horns of barges and the churning of the river. When it's foggy, they get so loud they wake up the birds who respond with piercing cries. And then you have to get up, and you see that the moon is full too, and the smell of river mud has barged in, thick and sensuous. And you put on the honey-silk voice of Aaron Neville who tells you that "it feels like rain." And you can be sure that it does, and that if someone is there next to you, you'll be making love.

And if no one is, you'll be immersed in that no-name regret, that bottomless longing for that nameless something. And if this isn't nature, then what can it be?

Nor does this feeling recede next morning when you walk the full three miles from your gardenia-smothered lair to Cafe du Monde for beignets and café au lait. The dawn has broken over the river. Both sides are gold: the steamboats and foreign ships on your side, and the West Bank on the opposite shore. The ships are floating above your head because you are under the river, a surreal perspective that never becomes routine. New Orleans is a bowl surrounded by levees: if they break, the bowl fills up and that's the end of us. Like Venice, Italy, this is a place of fleeting beauty. The knowledge that we won't be here long gives everyone an intense appetite for living. Or just an appetite: today, at Mike's On The Avenue, the special is Barbequed Oysters with Ginger and Pancetta. Recommended.

Someone living in the Louisiana bayous, in the Atchafalaya Basin, let's say, might meditate daily on the fragility of this river-built world. While pulling up his crab trap or digging for crawfish, he might wonder how long it will take the Mississippi to join up with his younger love, the swift Atchafalaya. Sooner or later they will because what the Old Man River wants the OMR gets. He might wonder also what he is doing in the annihilating heat of the day, prey to legions of insects and snakes as thick as spaghetti, when he could be in the cool mountains, lying flat on a boulder, surveying the valley below.

I think of that "someone" while I eat his superbly prepared catch and wonder what I am doing here, in a city of decay, crime, filth, and stench, when I could be in, let's say, Jerusalem, a city of ideas and stone.

New Orleans is in many ways the opposite of Jerusalem. It is most definitely not a holy city. The only religion that lays claim to the streets of the Vieux Carre is that ruled by Carnival, a cult of sensuousness, unconsciousness, dreams, masques, shifting identities, exaltation of the flesh. New Orleans is all flesh, Jerusalem is all spirit. This flesh of ours makes sounds, deep and mournful, or orgiastic and rapturous, sounds that are pre-articulate and too rich to be articulate. Jerusalem, on the other hand, laments and articulates, quarrels and specifies, laments and records. New Orleans is the slow-flowing mud of soul, Jerusalem the hard stones of spirit.

But one thing these cities have in common: they are both cemeteries. New Orleans, not nearly as old as Jerusalem, is yet a collection of graves surrounding the living. At St. Louis No. 1, for instance, you stand before the eroded angel and the iron cross at the grave of Monsieur Robert Armant, a Creole already dead in the last century, and wonder what relation if any he had to Camille Tainturier, her stone-flowers relief almost touching his. You put down your coffee on a broken urn and sit on his cracked stone, next to a wreath of plastic blue roses. Monsieur Robert was no Jesus, he founded no religion, but something about his dwelling place makes you think that he was a swashbuckling knight and a charming persuader, no less. Or maybe it's all wishful thinking: the "nature" of my mind.

The nature of New Orleans is to encourage the optimum development of New Orleanians: it's an environment for a specific life form, a dreamy, lazy, sentimental, musical one, prey to hallucinations (not visions), tolerant, indolent, and gifted at storytelling. This goes against the very grain of American "civilization" as we know it. We lie incongruously in the way of the thrifty, Puritan America whose concerns, including environmental ones, are driven by the logic of economies and planning. We, and our ways, are marked for elimination, there is no room in an efficient future for what we embody. Like the moon, we ought to be blown up, for interfering with the weather. This is a city of night, fog, and mud, the three elements against which all the might of America is mobilized.

The nature of New Orleans, I propose, is no less endangered than the nature of the Amazon. If the Amazon is to be protected—and I pray that it is—then we too ought to receive the same care. Our indefinable layering of sounds and sentimentalities should be defended against the endless suburbs spreading like mosquito clouds out of the swamps to the east. It should be, but by whom? Not, I hope, by the gratingly articulate bureaucrats of "heritage." Nor by those who would expand the metaphor of nature to take in cities. By whom then? By no one. If we are doomed—by the river or by something else—then so be it. This is how nature becomes natural.

Jane Hirshfield

Everything Alive

WHEN I WAS nineteen, I was asked in a dream, "Why do you write?" What came to mind at once was the place I grew up—a red brick project built on New York's Lower East Side to house veterans returning from World War II, each identical apartment building standing on a small scrap of lawn set off from the sidewalk by low swags of chain. And along with that image came the answer: "Because everything is alive." It was several years before I realized the seeming incongruity between image and answer, or even that the reply itself was something of a non sequitur. What I felt immediately, and still feel, was that the answer was true.

At the age of twenty-one, I did what many others like me

did in the late sixties or early seventies, in one variation or another: moved into a red Dodge van with a few beloved books, a camping stove and ice chest, a homemade wooden bed and tie-dyed curtains—my first and last sewing project—and started west. I stayed for a month in Boulder, for a few weeks in Santa Fe, but it was California that kept me.

I lived in San Francisco for a year, then with forty others in a narrow canyon in the midst of a national forest, where I listened for three years to the changing voices of a creek—its drought-hushed summer murmuring sometimes broken by the sharp love-talk of two mountain lions as they made their way downstream in the dark; its own water-lion roar in winter. The August meteor showers were followed faithfully by November rains, and the dusting of January snow on the ridge by thick-sprung wildflowers in April—Chinese houses, shooting stars, larkspur, the sticky monkey flowers sometimes more decorously called coral jewel weed.

There, though it is not the way I described to myself what I was doing, I did not write but studied the reason I had wanted to write. I knew very little, but I knew that I wanted to find the deep aliveness of beings and things I had glimpsed from time to time, but which mostly escaped me. I knew also that the only way toward that, for me, would be to find a way past the surface stories the self tells, a way through the self-turning I and into the eye that sees equally our own, human stories and the stories of manzanita and paintbrush and sage, of sandstone, of scrub jay, of star. And so I sat down and tried to learn how to pay attention, first to one thing—my own breathing—and then to everything, and when I left I took that intention with me, as much in my body as my mind.

I live now in a house with electricity, heat, hot water as well as cold, and in a more tamed landscape. The old-growth redwoods were cut long ago from the slopes of the mountain whose flank holds my home, though the second-growth is once again sieving rain from the coastal fog in my town. Two young redwoods are gradually taking the view across the valley from the bedroom window in a long, slow arboreal eclipse, but mostly the trees around me were brought in from elsewhere long ago: three aged apple, three pear, a plum, two apricot that struggle in the cool summer climate, and a fig that ripens perhaps one year out of four.

We cut out a vegetable bed from the small lawn, and reclaimed for hardy perennials the abandoned rock-lined flowerbeds we eventually found under their cover of invasive grasses and blackberry: now penstemon, lavender, rosemary, daylilies, and new South African imports—diascia, gaura—that can also do well in drought. And though this life is more protected than the elemental one of my early twenties, I try to remember in what I do here its lessons of permeability, of attention, of remaining close to where I am.

Negotiating with a quarter-acre of earth, I've found, is not unlike negotiating with the practice of meditation, or with a poem. First and last, you need to listen to the larger ground and life from which words, silence, and apples all arise, a ground that has its own givens, its own beauties, harshness, wisdom, and requirements. A good part of what I do in the garden would look (to put it in generous terms) like what the Taoists call *wu-wei:* the activity of not-doing. That means, in plain English, I mostly stand, or sit, looking either contemplative or lost, depending on the eye of the beholder.

I am an unabashedly lazy gardener and have never been very good at planning the future beyond what is absolutely necessary to order bulbs and seed, though I have read with pleasure the many books that recommend drawing up rotation charts or fertile, one-foot plots devoted to a single eggplant or a dozen scallions or three close-knit crowns of parsley. Instead, I stare, then one warm day when the sun's heat is the more luxurious for its autumn brevity, find myself racing for last July's harvest of garlic and shallots. I bring the basket out near a spot where the yellow squash plants thrived until the first cool nights blackened them back toward the soil they were made of, knowing that come spring this place will offer just the right amount of light for the new aromatic shoots to darken to a rich green. I estimate the effect of aged steer manure and other amendments I've rather casually shoveled in (something must always be added—to the ground, the concentrated products of chewed grass or burned wood or phosphate-rich rock; to a poem, whatever increase of being has been distilled from the hard and joyous voyages of heart and body and mind), and space the small bulbs accordingly, each planted to a depth determined by its own size.

Then I return to my own slow, composting observation made so gradually it is almost thoughtless, almost wordless. The foxgloves reseeding themselves for the second year running in the vegetable garden, among the gone-to-seed lettuce, are informing me of their preference for their own home— more humus, more moistness and shade: the climate of the Pacific Northwest, where I have seen them growing rampant by the roadsides. Through a kind of physical understanding, closer to dance than to language, I know that although they will grow and flower in the harsher location I've dictated (out of desire for a rising fountain of brown-speckled pinks outside the room where I write), it will always be a matter of discussion between us. To listen to them would be to save myself work each year, to allow the garden to more and more practice its own *wu-wei.* But sometimes, scarcely thinking about it, I choose the other, choose to make the effort to go in some small way against the nature of things as they are and toward the nature of imagination, of desire, which is also part of life, part of what Dylan Thomas called "the force that through the green fuse drives the flower."

There are many places in the world that should be left utterly alone and free of the effects of human will, but a garden is not one of them. In our encounter with any place, our ethical obligation is both to see it as it truly is and to imagine its most splendid fulfillment of being, and then to act toward and with it unselfishly, in accord with what we find. If we cultivate cities as cities, mountains as mountains, and our own minds and heart's desires as the half-wild, half-domesticated creatures that they are, perhaps we may yet make a way—late in the technological age though it is—toward a world alive and whole in all of its parts, and toward an appropriate humility in our relationship with it, whether in activity or in letting it be.

Today, after the first rains of October, new grass is coming up everywhere in the garden. I welcome it under the trees, pull it from between the young stands of red chard, and hope that both gestures are part of the work of attempting a human life that honors transience, interconnection, and praise. As weeding gardener, as revising writer, I sometimes think of the dictum of a sixth-century Chinese Zen master, Seng Ts'an: The perfect way is not difficult, only avoid picking and choosing.

But most of my life, it seems, rests somewhere between picking and choosing and understanding that the grass's return with the autumn rains is not a decision, is not willful, is not difficult as ordinary human life can, at times, seem difficult. And though my own being is no different from that of the nonhuman world, I weed, and write, and choose, and try to see the aliveness of the ten thousand grasses of each day a little more deeply, a little more precisely as I do, with gratitude for the wide field of red brick buildings and creek-speaking mountains and eternally returning blackberries that are equally the ground for it all.

Donald Hall

The One Hour

GOOD PLACES RAISE up their own time. For me, living in this New Hampshire house and landscape, morning is the best time. Most mornings I wake experimentally at two or three, check out the clock, and roll over. I want to get up and work, but I have learned: if I rise much before five, my out-of-whack day will never straighten itself.

November through February, I wake in deep darkness —the wrapped hive of blackness, image of the sole self—and read the paper drinking black coffee, then settle down to the desk as daylight suffuses gradually into frozen air. We live at the western foot of a hill, so the sky grays long before the sun arrives. Against that southern sky Mount Kearsarge rises first as a black outline. In late autumn it turns pink and lavender as the sun ascends; in winter the mountain looms bright white; then it greens slowly through spring into emerald summer. By June the birds wake before I do, making it impossible to stay in bed as they fill the ghost light with their early singing.

On a trip to India last fall I talked with a Bombay CEO who is also a novelist. He told me that he had recently addressed four hundred Indian businessmen on the subject of management, and in the question period a young man had asked him: "What is contentment?" (India's managers are not as America's.) He took two minutes to think, he told me, and then said that contentment was "absorbedness." As he told me this we mounted the stairs of excitement, agreeing with each other.

The hour of bliss is the lost hour. Love, physical love, absorbs the whole self like nothing else, but after a certain age it no longer engages the entire day. In this house on this land I lose the hour—inhabiting contentment—in my lucky double absorption with work and with land. At the desk, writing and trying to write, I do not know who I am; I do not even know that I will die. (Maybe *this* ignorance, which is bliss, explains the cathexis.) The whole of me enters the hand that holds the pen that digs at word-weeds, trying to set the garden straight. Who I am is what I do: activity is identity; and where I am—where I sit, what I see when I look out the window —lies under what I do.

Before I lived on this old family farm, I taught school in

Michigan and evaded absorbedness by wanting to be some-where else: New York or Wessex or Calcutta or New Hampshire. My clock ran by Standard American Time—the relentless thin suburban present, disconnected from the past, looking toward an illusory compensatory future. We only live in a true present when we thicken it with a real past and a possible future. Where I live now permits me the contentment of stasis, of being where and what I want to be, of concentration in the day's continuous moment.

My grandparents and great-grandparents lived here, worked hard with the absorbedness my Indian acquaintance spoke of. They dug real weeds, salted sheep, darned socks, harvested eggs, fenced pasture, canned Kentucky Wonders, hayed fields, and milked cows. They concentrated on what they did, like the old blacksmith at his forge or like the cousin who today tunes my car and pumps my gas. My neighbors who drive nails don't understand how I can sit still all day; but I couldn't shingle roofs all day, or dig wells, with competence or pleasure. (The neighbors and I agree: It takes all kinds.)

When I was a boy farming with my grandfather, I adored his loving and narrative company—but my farming days ended when a heart attack ended his. In my first years here I thought I should farm more than I did. I daydreamed immense vegetable gardens, made small ones and neglected them; canning and freezing vegetables, I longed for the desk. Now, I renounce guilt as I accept another assignment: to preserve in words—as much as I may—this house, this land, and this culture.

Place is all three. In 1975 I thought I had returned to a house of the beloved dead, but the moment I lived under the hill I understood that elms and boulders seized me as much as white clapboard did, or an old farmer's ghost. Then I discovered that my neighbors and cousins—people of stories and notions, people of speech cherished and passed along—split my grandfather into a million atoms and distributed him over hill-farms and villages through a hundred faces into a thousand laconic phrases.

By this time, the elms are as gone as the old-man farmers. Stone walls endure, tumbling apart as slowly as a mountain wears itself down. Where the settlers after the Revolution scrubbed out small farms, setting fieldstones into wavery rectangles, today mixed forests rise again amid glacial detritus. As the young people of the countryside grow middle-aged and old, they tell the story again—of one life in one locale, absorbed in its tender boundary.

Of course this place, and its consequent time, live under threat of assault from suburban armies. Ortega y Gassett predicted the vertical invasion of the barbarians; he did not predict that they would crash through the wall driving Buicks. Good places are under continual threat, and the one hour is always precarious.

Contributors

ALISON BAKER lives in southwestern Oregon. Her most recent book is *Loving Wanda Beaver: Novella and Stories* (Chronicle Books, 1995). She won first prize in the 1994 O. Henry Prize Story collection for "Better Be Ready 'Bout Half Past Eight," which was part of her first collection of short stories, *How I Came West, and Why I Stayed* (Chronicle Books, 1994).

LYNNE BAMA writes about nature and the environment from her home in northwestern Wyoming. Her essays and articles have appeared in *Sierra, Orion, Rocky Mountain, Northern Lights,* and *High Country News.* She is working on a book about the original people of Yellowstone National Park.

M. GARRETT BAUMAN is a professor of English and human ecology at Monroe Community College in Rochester, New York. He is the author of *Ideas and Details* (Harcourt Brace, 1992) and *The Shape of Ideas* (Harcourt Brace, 1995), and received a 1995 New York State Foundation for the Arts award for nature writing. His essays on nature and education have appeared in *The New York Times, Yankee, National Forum, Sierra,* and other journals.

ANDREI CODRESCU teaches English at Louisiana State University and is a frequent commentator on National Public Radio. He has written more than twenty books of poetry, fiction, and essays; his new books are *The Blood Countess* (Simon & Schuster, 1995) and *Cyber Nowhere* (St. Martin's Press, 1996). He is the editor of *Exquisite Corpse: A Journal of Books & Ideas* in New Orleans and Baton Rouge.

ROBERT CRUM is a photographer and writer who recently moved to Oregon after living in Florida for six years. His essays have appeared in *Wilderness* and *Wildlife Conservation,* and he is the author of a children's book on Native American powwows, *Eagle Drum* (Macmillan, 1994). He is currently working on a book about kids in rodeos.

JOHN DANIEL is the author of two books of poems, *Common Ground* (Confluence Press, 1988) and *All Things Touched by Wind* (Salmon Run Press, 1994), and *The Trail Home* (Pantheon, 1994), a collection of essays on nature, imagination, and the American West. He is poetry editor of *Wilderness* magazine. "Turnings of Seasons," the piece he wrote for "Whereabouts" in 1992, has been revised and expanded for this collection and has further mutated into a book-length memoir, *Toward Oregon,* which will be published in 1996 by Counterpoint.

ALISON HAWTHORNE DEMING is the director of the Poetry Center at the University of Arizona. She received the 1993

Walt Whitman Award for *Science and Other Poems* (Louisiana State University Press, 1994). Her collection of essays, *Temporary Homelands,* was published in 1994 by Mercury House.

DAVID GUTERSON's first novel, *Snow Falling on Cedars* (Vintage, 1995), won the 1994 PEN-Faulkner Award. He is the author of a collection of short stories, *The Country Ahead of Us, the Country Behind* (Vintage, 1996), and a contributing editor to *Harper's.*

JOHN HAINES is a recent recipient of a literary award from the American Academy of Art and Letters, and is currently Visiting Associate Professor at the University of Hawaii, Manoa. His latest book is a collection of essays, *Fables and Distances* (Graywolf Press, 1995). His collected poems, *The Owl in the Mask of the Dreamer,* was published by Graywolf in 1993.

DONALD HALL has written thirteen books of poetry, most recently *The Museum of Clear Ideas* (Ticknor & Fields, 1993). His many books of prose include *Life Work* (Beacon Press, 1993) and *Principal Products of Portugal* (Farrar, Straus & Giroux, 1995).

SUE HALPERN is the author of *Migrations to Solitude* (Vintage, 1993) and a contributor to many journals and magazines. She is currently at work on a new book.

GERALD HASLAM has published seven collections of short stories, the most recent of which is *Condor Dreams and Other Fiction* (University of Nevada Press, 1994). He has written and edited several books of nonfiction, and teaches English at California State University-Sonoma.

JANE HIRSHFIELD has written three collections of poetry, most recently *The October Palace* (HarperCollins, 1994).

She has also edited an anthology, *Women in Praise of the Sacred* (HarperCollins, 1994), and co-translated a collection of Japan's two foremost women poets, *The Ink Dark Moon* (Vintage, 1990). She has received a Guggenheim Fellowship, the Bay Area Book Reviewers Award, and a Pushcart Prize. A student of Zen since 1974, she has taught poetry at the University of California at Berkeley and at the University of San Francisco.

PAM HOUSTON moved to the San Francisco Bay Area in 1994 from Park City, Utah. She is the author of a collection of short stories, *Cowboys Are My Weakness* (Washington Square Press, 1993), and is currently working on a novel, a screenplay, and a collection of essays.

CATHY JOHNSON is a naturalist, artist, and author of more than twenty books, including *The Sierra Club Guide to Sketching in Nature* (Sierra Club Books, 1990). She is staff naturalist for *Country Living* magazine and a columnist for *The Artist's Magazine.*

GENE LOGSDON, with his wife, Carol, lives and works on a small farm in Ohio. He is the author of some fourteen books, the latest being *At Nature's Pace* (Pantheon, 1994) and *The Contrary Farmer* (Chelsea Green Publishing, 1994). An award-winning newspaper columnist, he is a contributing editor to *Ohio* and *BioCycle* magazines and has written numerous articles for many other publications.

NANCY LORD is the author of two collections of short fiction, including *Survival* (Coffee House Press, 1991). Her essays have appeared in *Sierra, Manōa, Left Bank, Alaska Quarterly Review,* and elsewhere, and have been widely anthologized. Her latest work, *Fishcamp: Mapping a Home Place,* further explores the history, natural history, and personal history around the area described in "A Crying Country."

TIM MCNULTY has written five books of poetry and eight books of natural history, including an award-winning series on national parks coauthored with photographer Pat O'Hara. His most recent book of poems is *In Blue Mountain Dusk* (Broken Moon Press, 1992). His guide to the natural history of Olympic National Park was published by Houghton Mifflin in 1995.

CHRISTOPHER MERRILL'S works include *Watch Fire* (White Pine, 1994) and several other collections of poems, and the nonfiction book *The Grass of Another Country: A Journey Through the World of Soccer* (Henry Holt, 1993). He is the editor of *The Forgotten Language: Contemporary Poets and Nature* (Peregrine Smith Books, 1991). His newest books are a translation of Ales Debeljak's *Anxious Moments* (White Pine, 1994) and *The Old Bridge: The Third Balkan War and the Age of the Refugee* (Milkweed, 1995).

W. S. MERWIN, who received the Pulitzer Prize for poetry in 1970 for *The Carrier of Ladders,* has written numerous books of poetry and prose, including *The Rain in the Trees* (Knopf, 1988) and *The Lost Upland* (Henry Holt, 1993). His most recent collection of poems is *Travels* (Knopf, 1992).

KATHLEEN NORRIS is the author of *Dakota: A Spiritual Geography* (Houghton Mifflin, 1993) and several books of poetry, including *Little Girls in Church* (University of Pittsburgh, 1995). A new book of essays entitled *The Cloister Walk* will be published by Riverhead/Putnam's in early 1997.

BRENDA PETERSON has written three novels, *River of Light* (Knopf, 1978), *Becoming the Enemy* (Graywolf Press, 1988), and *Duck and Cover* (HarperCollins, 1991), as well as two collections of essays, *Living by Water* (Fawcett/Columbine, 1994) and *Nature and Other Mothers* (HarperCollins, 1992). Her sixth book, *Sister Stories; Taking the Journey Together,* was published early this year by Viking/Penguin.

REYNOLDS PRICE is James B. Duke Professor of English at Duke University and has published numerous novels, collections of stories, poems, plays, essays, and translations. He is a member of the American Academy of Arts and Letters, and his work has appeared in sixteen languages.

GARY SNYDER is a poet, essayist, and watershed activist. His most recent book of poems is *No Nature* (Pantheon, 1992), and a collection of new and selected essays, *A Place in Space,* was published by Counterpoint in 1995. He lives in the northern California Sierra Nevada and manages trees for the Yuba Watershed Institute and papers for the University of California at Davis.

MARY SOJOURNER lives outside Flagstaff, Arizona, where she writes and conducts workshops in short fiction and nature writing. The author of a novel, *Sisters of the Dream* (Northland, 1989), she has won several regional and national awards for her short stories and essays. She is currently working on *Going Through Ghosts,* a novel about the Vietnam War.

KEN WRIGHT has worked as a park ranger, hydrologist, river guide, and newspaper reporter, and is the author of *A Wilder Life; Essays from Home* (Kivaki Press, 1995). He lives in the San Juan Mountains of Colorado, where he is a free-lance writer, college instructor, husband, and father of two.